Equipment Sustainment Requirements
for the Transforming Army

Eric Peltz

Prepared for the United States Army

RAND

Arroyo Center

The research described in this report was sponsored by the United States Army under Contract No. DASW01-01-C-0003.

Library of Congress Cataloging-in-Publication Data

Peltz, Eric, 1968–
    Equipment Sustainment Requirements for the Transforming Army / Eric Peltz.
      p. cm.
    "MR-1577."
    ISBN 0-8330-3205-4
    1. United States. Army—Operational readiness. 2. United States. Army—Equipment—Quality control. 3. United States. Army—Supplies and stores. I.Title.

UA25 .P35 2003
355.8'0973—dc21

                                          2002075192

RAND is a nonprofit institution that helps improve policy and decisionmaking through research and analysis. RAND® is a registered trademark. RAND's publications do not necessarily reflect the opinions or policies of its research sponsors.

Cover design by Peter Soriano

Published 2003 by RAND
1700 Main Street, P.O. Box 2138, Santa Monica, CA 90407-2138
1200 South Hayes Street, Arlington, VA 22202-5050
201 North Craig Street, Suite 202, Pittsburgh, PA 15213
RAND URL: http://www.rand.org/
To order RAND documents or to obtain additional information, contact Distribution Services: Telephone: (310) 451-7002; Fax: (310) 451-6915; Email: order@rand.org

Over the last several years, a vision of the future U.S. Army has begun to crystallize in revolutionary new Objective Force operational concepts and capabilities that will place an unprecedented combination of performance expectations, constraints, and demanding conditions on combat service support (CSS). For example, highly mobile forces with reduced CSS structures will have to be sustained at high levels of operational availability, often while being widely distributed across a battlefield. The resulting challenge has triggered examinations of how equipment sustainment requirements should be defined in developing materiel requirements for new weapon systems.

The Assistant Secretary of the Army for Acquisition, Logistics, and Technology (ASA[ALT]) asked RAND Arroyo Center to assess how the Army should define equipment sustainment requirements, what methods and tools equipment developers might need to use these requirements effectively, and which, if any, have merit as key performance parameters. This report presents the conclusions. The research was carried out as part of a project sponsored by the ASA(ALT) to examine the implications of a hybrid force of legacy, recapitalized, and new systems for equipment sustainment capabilities and the consequent effects on mission effectiveness and resource requirements.

The report should interest the Army's acquisition community, logisticians, materiel requirements developers, and operational leaders. This research was carried out in the Military Logistics Program of RAND Arroyo Center, a federally funded research and development center sponsored by the United States Army.

For more information on RAND Arroyo Center, contact the Director of Operations (telephone 310-393-0411, extension 6500; FAX 310-451-6952; e-mail donnab@rand.org), or visit the Arroyo Center's Web site at http://www.rand.org/ard/.

CONTENTS

FIGURES

TABLES

SUMMARY

A central goal of the Army Transformation is a large reduction in the amount of combat service support (CSS) personnel and equipment—the CSS footprint—in the combat zone. Reduced footprint will enhance not only strategic mobility through increased deployment speed but also operational and tactical mobility, key parts of emerging Objective Force operational concepts that envision a fast-paced, nonlinear battlefield with forces rapidly shifting across large distances. The wide dispersion of units and unsecure lines of communication that will result from these envisioned nonlinear operations lead to a second goal: self-sufficient maneuver units during operational "pulses."[1]

To achieve these goals, the Army must improve the supportability of future systems and the effectiveness of the logistics system, which together determine the sustainability of the Army's weapon systems.[2] To drive such improvements, the Army needs to identify an effective set of equipment sustainment requirements for weapon system

---

[1]For a discussion of future Army warfighting concepts and force requirements, see "Concepts for the Objective Force," United States Army White Paper, 2001. Support footprint goals are found in "The Army's CS/CSS Transformation: Executive Summary," Briefing, January 21, 2000.

[2]Supportability, a characteristic of weapon systems that can be influenced to the greatest degree in early design stages, is a measure of the amount and nature of resources needed to support a weapon system. It consists of reliability, maintainability, and durability. "Equipment sustainment capability" in this report is defined as the Army's ability to keep equipment operational from a maintenance standpoint. It is driven by two factors: equipment supportability and logistics system capabilities. Other sustainment capabilities, such as providing fuel, ammunition, and water, are not treated in this report.

programs that are aligned with Objective Force operational concepts. To assist with this task, the Assistant Secretary of the Army for Acquisition, Logistics, and Technology (ASA[ALT]) asked RAND Arroyo Center to develop a set of metrics to define equipment sustainment requirements and to assess their potential merit as key performance parameters (KPPs).

WHY DOES THE ARMY'S EQUIPMENT SUPPORTABILITY NEED IMPROVEMENT?

Poor supportability exacts substantial costs: low mission availability, a large maintenance footprint, and high maintenance costs. Although Army readiness rates averaged across time and units often meet or exceed Army goals (90 percent for ground systems and 75 percent for aviation), the reality of equipment availability is more complex. During battalion-level training exercises, daily not-mission-capable (NMC) rates frequently climb above 20 percent, and daily battalion-level NMC rates as high as 45 percent have been observed for M1A1 Abrams tanks—despite the presence of a large maintenance footprint. Maintainers currently make up close to 20 percent of the personnel in both Army of Excellence and Force XXI heavy divisions, and about 15 percent of the personnel in task-organized heavy brigade combat teams. And the costs of maintenance are high: in 1999, for example, the Army spent about $8.5 billion, or more than 12 percent of its budget, to maintain equipment.

THE GOALS OF EQUIPMENT SUSTAINMENT

The Army's desire to reduce the costs of poor supportability reflects in three overarching equipment sustainment goals: high availability during combat pulses, small maintenance footprint, and low maintenance costs. In the course of the Objective Force concept development, the Army has added another goal: maneuver force self-sufficiency, that is, operating without external support or resupply during surges of continuous operations or "combat pulses." Pulses have been defined as three days of continuous combat in mid- to high-intensity conflict, and seven days of continuous operation in low-end conflict.[3]

The aggressiveness of the Army's Transformation goals is leading to new force designs with substantially reduced maintenance footprint. For example, in the Interim Division (draft) and the Stryker Brigade Combat Team (SBCT) designs, the ratios of maintainers to total personnel are about a half and a third, respectively, of heavy division and brigade combat team ratios. Moreover, the Future Combat Systems (FCS) concept, envisioned as a system of highly interdependent systems, implies a need for higher-than-ever availability for some system elements; draft FCS-based unit designs target much lower maintenance footprint than even the SBCT. Achieving the aggressive CSS Transformation goals will require changes not only in logistics structures and processes but also in the nature and amount of demands placed upon the logistics system by the Army's equipment— the supportability of systems that results from the requirements development, concept development, engineering design, engineering development, and testing processes. Thus, the requirements and acquisition processes must play key roles in the CSS Transformation.

EQUIPMENT SUSTAINMENT REQUIREMENTS

When an acquisition program begins, the Army should first assess how mission needs influence the relative importance of each overarching equipment sustainment goal, along with desired levels of performance. This assessment will help identify any potential KPPs that should be emphasized during concept and technology development and will facilitate the comparison of various concepts. Table S.1 provides a potential template for the overall goals and associated metrics. These are high-level equipment sustainment requirements that directly reflect operational and overall Army needs. The middle column provides generic requirements or program goals associated with each high-level requirements category, and the far right column provides metrics for defining the requirements and setting objective and threshold values.

---

[3]DARPA Solicitation No. PS 02-07, DARPA/Army FCS Program, Competitive Solicitation, Defense Advanced Research Projects Agency.

Table S.1

Overall Equipment Sustainment Program Goals and Metrics

Requirement Category	Equipment Sustainment Program Goals	Potential Standard Metrics for Defining Sustainment Requirements
Availability	• Meet mission needs • Maximize pulse availability • Maximize sortie availability (as applicable)	• Pulse A_o (operational availability) — Use derived pulse A_i in some cases • Prob(successful sortie completion) (as applicable) • Specify pulse, refit, and sortie parameters[a]
Self-sufficiency	• Unit self-sufficiency during pulses	• Self-sufficiency pulse length
Equipment sustainment footprint	• Minimize deployment footprint and maneuver force footprint	• Maintainers by echelon (cost and footprint driver); or maintenance ratio by echelon • Maintenance equipment lift requirements
Life cycle equipment sustainment cost	• Minimize life cycle cost	• Total life cycle cost to "maintain" • Annual operation (cost per operating hour/mile) • Planned recapitalization • Spare parts provisioning • Investment in reliability (e.g., materiel)

[a]Critical assumptions that are necessary to determine the associated requirements.

To measure the ability to keep equipment available for use during combat or other operations—the ultimate purpose of equipment sustainment—the Army should employ the metric pulse operational availability (A_o). Pulse A_o is defined in this document as the percentage of time a system is available over the course of a combat pulse, which is equivalent to the probability that the system is operational at any point in time during a pulse. An alternative form of a pulse A_o requirement would be to specify the minimum A_o that must be maintained over the course of a combat pulse by a unit—call this minimum pulse A_o. It would be defined as the probability that availability remains above a threshold for an entire pulse. This would be important when a minimum level is deemed necessary to maintain a unit's combat effectiveness. Pulse A_o, in one or both of these forms, is what commanders care about.

In cases where the pulse A_o is to be achieved without external support, self-sufficiency should be an overall goal. Self-sufficiency from a maintenance standpoint is defined as a period during which an organization will operate without resupply of spare parts or maintenance support from units that are not part of the maneuver force. To achieve a desired level of A_o, self-sufficiency has implications for the required levels of reliability and maintainability and the amount of spare parts and the maintenance capacity within a maneuver force.

From the pulse A_o requirement, between-pulse recovery assumptions, the self-sufficiency requirement, reliability requirements, combat damage rate assumptions, and maintainability requirements, the Army can determine the maintenance capacity in terms of personnel and equipment necessary at each echelon. Alternatively, these capacity requirements could be fixed if the desire is to constrain footprint to a certain level, and then one or more of the other requirements could be derived. Two simple footprint metrics—the number of maintenance personnel by echelon (or the maintenance ratio) and the lift requirements for equipment by echelon—should be sufficient. The number of personnel and the amount of equipment they have create demand for strategic lift, intratheater lift for nonlinear operations, and sustainment resources (water, food, fuel, food service personnel, medical personnel, force protection, etc.).

Total life cycle cost related to equipment sustainment should include annual maintenance support costs, initial spare parts provisioning, and any planned recapitalization or overhaul costs. It could also include design-driven costs when design decisions made solely to improve reliability or maintainability increase cost. Such design characteristics could include component or subsystem redundancy, more robust components, failure-prevention sensors, new materials, and built-in prognostic or diagnostic sensors and automation.

Once a concept is selected for full development, successful program development will require supplementing the broad, overarching goals (equipment pulse availability, maintenance footprint, self-sufficiency, and cost) with a set of detailed, "one-dimensional," directly measurable requirements, based on the design assumptions of the concept, that can provide performance feedback and accountability throughout the development of the weapon system. For equipment sustainment, we have laid out a set of metrics (see Table S.2) along the functional dimensions of reliability, maintainability, fleet life cycle management, and supply support that, when employed in conjunction with the overarching goals, will indicate whether the program is making the desired progress.

Reliability is critical to all four overarching goals for two reasons: its effect on a force's ability to accomplish missions and its effect on the resources, in terms of cost and footprint, required to restore and sustain weapon systems. The effect of reliability on mission accomplishment can be measured in terms of mean time between critical failures (MTBCF).[4] Although critical failures are of the most interest to operators because they can affect mission accomplishment, logisticians are concerned also with noncritical failures, because every failure produces resource demands. Thus it is imperative to measure mean time between maintenance actions (MTBM), which should be divided into MTBUM (unscheduled maintenance—what we think of when things break) and MTBSM (scheduled maintenance—what we think of when we bring our cars in for service or when we schedule a tank for overhaul), because they place different types of demands on the logistics system in terms of total resources and the ability to control when they occur.

Maintainability encompasses factors that affect the resources and time needed to complete repairs—including diagnosis and actual work—and capabilities that enable the logistics system to keep failures from affecting operations. Important questions are: How long does it take to do the repair work ("wrench-turning time")? How much training is needed to complete repairs? What special tools and equipment are needed? The answers to these questions are affected,

---

[4]In this document, a critical failure is defined as a failure that makes a piece of equipment NMC.

Table S.2

Equipment Sustainment Functional Design Objectives and Metrics

Requirement Category	Equipment Sustainment Functional Design Objectives	Potential Standard Metrics for Defining Equipment Sustainment Requirements
Reliability	• Minimize mission-critical failures • Minimize maintenance requirements	• Standard form of MTBCF • MTBUM and MTBSM (by echelon)
Maintainability	• Prevent faults from becoming mission critical • Minimize downtime and cost • Minimize maintenance footprint and cost • Minimize maintenance footprint forward	• FFSP = Fn(FFP, FIR, FAR/NEOF Rate) • FFSD = Fn(FFD, FIR, FAR/NEOF Rate) • MTTR (by echelon) • MMH/UM (by echelon) • MMH/SM (by echelon) • Percent UM-crew, org, DS, GS
Fleet life cycle management	• Recognize life cycle costs up front • Account for life cycle operations	• Specify replacement/recap/retirement schedule • Use estimate of reliability degradation in requirements analysis[a]
Supply support	• Minimize CWT • Minimize cost and footprint	• Local fill rate • Battle damage parts kit • Wholesale backorder rate • Percent of parts that are unique • Number and positioning of end item "spares" • Specify ALDT assumption[a]

[a]Critical assumptions that are necessary to determine the associated requirements.

in part, by how components and subsystems, whichever represent the desired level of replacement, are packaged within the total system. For example, how easy are they to get to (accessibility)? Another key maintainability area is the quality of troubleshooting procedures, whether fully automated through sensors and built-in tests, completely manual using paper technical manuals, or something in between. Quickly diagnosing a problem and getting the diagnosis right the first time can have a big effect on repair time, and the knowledge required for diagnosis determines who potentially can do maintenance.

Besides reducing total workload (total footprint and costs) and affecting workload distribution (footprint distribution), maintainability can play a role in reducing mission-critical failures, thereby improving pulse A_o, through prognostic technology that makes anticipatory maintenance feasible. The Army is making strong efforts to encourage the development and use of prognostics. The benefit of prognostics, though, is limited by the percentage of faults that can be successfully predicted, which should be measured if prognostics are viewed as a key part of a system concept.

Beyond affecting total force structure requirements, better maintainability can reduce footprint in the maneuver force. For example, if crews can repair a large percentage of faults, it would reduce both the overall need for maintainers as well as those in the maneuver force. To encourage this, a metric such as the percentage of unscheduled maintenance actions that can be accomplished by the crew could be used. Expressly designing new weapon systems to take advantage of new support concepts will further enhance their effectiveness and value.

Fleet life cycle management considerations include supportability degradation over time (how quickly does a system wear?) and the planned actions to maintain equipment performance at its design capability. Such requirements should be explicitly recognized up front in program planning and resource allocation. Computing a meaningful life cycle cost requires a reasonable, supportable estimate of life cycle length. Any needs for recapitalization or major overhaul programs based on this life cycle length should be explicitly forecast and recognized as a program requirement. Additionally, to the degree that reasonable means can be found to develop such estimates, degradation in system failure rates from wear over time should be accounted for—both in evaluating life cycle cost and determining reliability requirements.

In general, the spare parts supply chain that provides supply support is thought of as a broad system designed by the Army and Department of Defense (DoD) to support all weapon systems, so it is not generally thought of as an area that should have program-specific requirements. However, some systems are so significant or important to the Army's future that they may drive the entire support structure to begin a transition toward a new support concept. Similarly, a system may represent the first in a new generation of weapon systems that will necessitate a new support concept. From this vantage point, the support structure becomes integral to the total weapon system concept, and thus the Army may want to include in the program's requirements any changes to the structure that are critical to the concept's success.

Aside from this, program requirements always rest on some assumptions, often with regard to parts support. A key element of parts support that drives much of the differences in total repair time among weapon systems and units is local inventory performance. Programs should set local fill rate performance requirements that support any assumptions made in the requirements determination process. Similarly, a level of wholesale spare parts performance could be specified. And one element of weapon system design that the Army can use as a lever for reducing the resource requirements necessary to provide a given level of parts support is part commonality.

THE CRITICALITY OF ASSUMPTIONS

To measure progress toward achieving the overarching goals, each of the potential standard metrics identified for defining equipment sustainment requirements needs to be decomposed into its root-level design elements. For example, pulse operational availability (A_o), which measures the percentage of time a system is available over the course of a combat pulse, is a function of two root metrics: the mission-critical failure rate and the total time required to return items to mission-capable status. For pulse A_o to be a viable metric, these root metrics have to be reliably estimable.

Producing reliable estimates, and the generation of effective sustainment requirements in general, depends critically on good assumptions. For example, calculating pulse A_o requires an assumption about the average total broke-to-fix time. An unrealistically optimistic broke-to-fix time assumption will lead to a much lower reliability requirement to meet a given pulse A_o and would produce a misleading assessment of pulse A_o. When fielded, such a system would then experience lower-than-desired pulse A_o.

ASSESSING THE MERITS OF MAKING EQUIPMENT SUSTAINMENT REQUIREMENTS KPPs

Given that equipment sustainment is so vital to Objective Force concepts, the question arises as to whether, and if so which, equipment sustainment requirements should be designated as KPPs. Such designation brings about congressional oversight and can trigger legally required program reviews. In general, KPPs should be those *precise* requirements (i.e., thresholds) that—if not met—should cause the managing service or DoD to consider dramatically changing or even canceling a program. To ensure that their use is aligned with this KPP concept, DoD and the Army have designed policy criteria for determining which requirements should be KPPs in terms of both intent and practicality. The intent criteria define what the KPPs are meant to represent from a theoretical standpoint (e.g., basic definition of a system, mission essentiality, sole means of achieving critical operational goal), while the practical criteria ensure that KPPs are useful and supportable in practice (i.e., technical and financial feasibility, existence of a justifiable threshold, and reliable assessability).

All four of the overarching logistics and readiness goals—pulse A_o, footprint, self-sufficiency, and life cycle sustainment costs—have potential merit as KPPs from an intent standpoint, while one-dimensional functional design requirements have less potential because they are typically not the sole means of achieving a critical operational goal. For example, pulse A_o would be a viable KPP if the mission need dictates that some minimum level of availability is necessary for mission accomplishment (the point at which a force becomes combat ineffective).

What the Army must decide is whether, for a given weapon system, one or more of these sustainability requirements are absolutely essential for it to have value. In addition, it should be remembered that the KPP decision is ultimately about which *feasible* characteristics are essential. As such, some requirements might only achieve KPP potential if their feasibility reaches a level that provides a whole new type of operational capability that produces a step change in overall performance. Thus a desire for an aggressive advance in performance should be reflected as a KPP only if the entire value of a system depends on whether such an aggressive advance can be achieved. Otherwise, the Army should rigorously pursue an increase in the feasible level through research investments and contractor incentives without making the program depend on achieving the "stretch goal."

THE ENTIRE TRADESPACE SHOULD BE CONSIDERED DURING CONCEPT DEVELOPMENT

Initially, the Army considered Objective Force concepts that would have required combat pulse self-sufficiency without any maintenance personnel in the maneuver force. To make such a concept feasible would require very high FCS pulse reliability—such as 90 to 95 percent for a three-day high-intensity pulse—to achieve desired levels of equipment availability.[5] To meet this goal even at an individual system level (let alone a networked system of systems), the Army would have to achieve dramatic improvement over current levels of reliability. Equipment availability performance at the National Training Center (NTC) illustrates the type of improvement needed. A seven-day pulse is used for comparison to account for the higher operating tempo envisioned for an Objective Force pulse. In five NTC rotations during fiscal years 2000 and 2001, the seven-day pulse reliability for M1A2s averaged 58 percent, which means that it would require a fivefold increase in the MTBCF for M1A2s to achieve a 90 percent seven-day pulse reliability operating at a NTC-like level of intensity. Over the past two years, battalions with NTC prepositioned M1A1s and home-station M1A1s averaged only 37 percent seven-day pulse reliability (with home-station M1A1s actually performing below this average) and would therefore require about a ninefold increase in MTBCF to reach 90 percent pulse reliability. And if combat damage were added to these failures as part of an overall suitability analysis, it would potentially drive the need for even greater reliability. Numbers for the somewhat simpler M2 Bradley have been a little better but still present a substantial gap, with the reliability of relatively new Bradleys just one-fourth that needed to achieve 90 percent seven-day pulse reliability at NTC.

It will probably be difficult to close this gap in one generation of weapon system development, particularly because reliability im-

---

[5]Pulse reliability is defined as the probability that a system will remain mission capable for an entire combat pulse of defined length.

provements are typically process-driven rather than achieved through revolutionary "silver bullet" technological solutions. Dramatic improvements in reliability require improving a host of subsystems and thousands of dissimilar components (e.g., hydraulics, electronics, mechanical parts, and sensors). Technology solutions are certainly possible, but they could result in higher cost (expensive electronics, sensors, advanced materials, or redundancy) or weight (e.g., beefier suspension components), which could require tradeoffs in deployability or fuel efficiency.

The reliability gap between current systems and those needed to achieve the envisioned Objective Force concepts can begin to narrow if the Army were to allow for a broader "tradespace" to achieve availability goals by balancing overarching equipment sustainment goals against each other. For example, to achieve pulse A_0 performance levels similar to those of the M1A2-equipped battalions at NTC over the course of a rotation (indicated by line 1 in Figure S.1)—but without any repair capability—an increase in reliability of an order of magnitude would be required, as illustrated by line 3. However, a similar pulse A_0 could be achieved with a still substantial but more modest twofold MTBCF improvement and a 50 percent reduction in repair capacity (line 4). This balanced, and likely more feasible, approach would still reduce the maintenance footprint substantially. Moreover, maintainability improvements could further reduce the necessary repair capacity and footprint, perhaps to a level 75 percent lower than today's, with this same MTBCF improvement. The Army should pursue aggressive improvements and innovations across several means of keeping equipment available, because it would be risky to rely on just one method to reach the high pulse A_0 that the FCS should have while also reaching the other overarching goals. In fact, through this type of tradespace exploration, many in the Army are realizing the potential inherent in each of the sustainment levers. They have realized that this type of approach will probably be more effective than relying on reliability alone. Increasingly, attention is being focused more broadly on availability, with a recognition that reliability, maintainability, fleet life cycle management, and supply performance must all improve substantially to reach overall FCS goals.

In conclusion, adopting a standard set of potential requirements and associated metrics for consideration by every program will help the

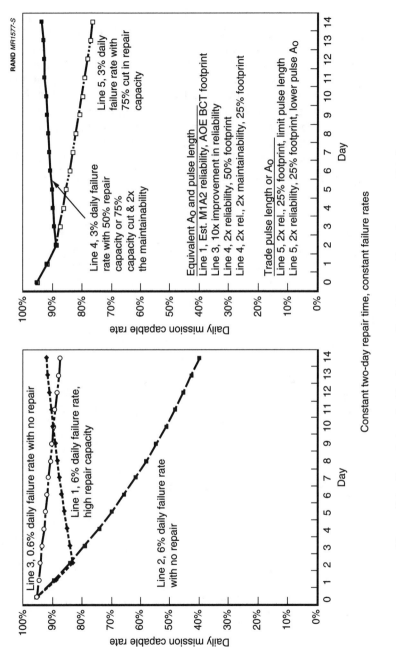

Figure S.1—Examining the Equipment Sustainment Requirements Tradespace

Army address the full spectrum of overarching goals and design objectives for equipment sustainment—provided that good assumptions are employed in the requirements determination process. In conjunction, the Army should review several overarching sustainability requirements to assess their desirability as KPPs. These requirements do not necessarily need to be limited to maintenance sustainment alone; they could include all sustainment requirements. Finally, beyond the option of designating one or more equipment sustainment requirements as KPPs, the Army should explore the potential value of additional policies and strategies to provide incentives for improved equipment sustainment performance.

ACKNOWLEDGMENTS

I thank the Honorable Paul Hoeper, then Assistant Secretary of the Army for Acquisition, Logistics, and Technology (ASA[ALT]), and his staff for sponsoring this research in response to their recognition of the critical importance of ensuring that the Army's requirement and acquisition processes are aligned with new Objective Force concepts from an equipment sustainment perspective. Within the Office of the ASA(ALT), I thank Dr. Walter Morrison, the Director for Research and Laboratory Management, for taking on management responsibility for the project. His valuable feedback on draft briefings significantly sharpened the research. His action officers, initially Ms. Suzanne Kirchoff and later Mr. Joseph Flesch, have assisted in scoping the research and coordinating information and feedback briefings.

Within the Army, many people have provided critical information about the requirements development and acquisition processes. In particular, I wish to thank Mr. Michael Harvey, Chief of the Combat Developments Engineering (CDE) Division of the Training and Doctrine Command's (TRADOC) Requirements Integration Directorate, his two Regional Managers, Mr. Terry DeWitt and Mr. Merrill Williams, and Mr. Jeffrey Higgins, a Senior Engineer in the CDE Division, for providing insight into the requirements determination process through interviews, requirements documentation from past programs, and instructional material as well as feedback on an early draft of this briefing. Mr. Steve French, Chief of Systems Engineering in the Office of the ASA(ALT), helped build upon this insight through discussions of current issues in requirements policy and offered valuable suggestions for research directions.

Additionally, several people in the office of the Program Manager, Abrams Tank Systems, and the office of the TRADOC System Manager, Abrams Tank Systems, clarified how the requirements development and changes processes actually work in practice.

Compiling the estimate of the Army's cost of maintenance in fiscal year 1999 required the assistance of many people. Several members of the Army Budget Office were instrumental in ensuring that I used the correct budget numbers to estimate Army maintenance costs. And at RAND, Dr. Ellen Pint provided financial documents and, along with Dr. Christopher Hanks, provided an education on Army Working Capital Fund budgets. Also at RAND, Mr. Charles Kaylor provided information on the Army's personnel databases and coordinated with Lieutenant Colonel Paul Thorton and Mr. Mike Carty in the Office of the Deputy Chief of Staff, G-1, to get data extracts from PERTAADS. Mr. Art Lackey assisted in developing the estimate of supply personnel in the Army in support of maintenance, Mr. William O'Malley extracted military and civilian maintenance personnel numbers from DoD databases, and Mr. Bruce Held provided data on Army maintenance contracts from previous research he had conducted.

Captains Brandon Grubbs and Chris Dexter, Observer-Controllers at the National Training Center, provided detailed data, which they manually record every day during each rotation. The data have become valuable in helping us better understand the drivers of equipment readiness in the U.S. Army.

In addition to being a source of research information, many people in the Army have taken the time to receive draft briefings and give feedback. Along with Dr. Morrison, Dr. Robert S. Rohde, his Deputy Director for Laboratory Management, and Ms. Deborah Pollard-Reed of the Logistics Integration Agency (LIA) critiqued a series of draft briefings and helped ensure that the research was progressing in directions valuable to the Army. Ms. Pollard-Reed also coordinated written comments on the subject area from experts in the Office of the Army's Deputy Chief of Staff, G-4 and then volunteered to coordinate broad vetting of the research through a series of briefings.

Within the staff office of the Army's G-4, BG Barbara Doornink, Colonels Don Plater, Robert Kleba, Robert Klass, Joe Albright, Ed

Morehead, and Mathias Velasco, Mr. Larry Hill, LTC Robin Stauffer, and LTC Janice Ferguson received the briefing and provided constructive comments. BG Doornink also sponsored the research to LTG Charles Mahan, the Army's DCS G-4, and MG Daniel Mongeon, Director of Sustainment, DCS G-4. I appreciate the help of Mr. Roger Hamerlinck, the G-4 action officer, on many areas of this research, with in-depth communication of the issues of concern to the staff. In addition to the logisticians on the Army Staff, I am grateful for the feedback of COL Larry Harman, Mr. Robert Dienes, MAJ Al Morgan, CPT Paul Landry, and Mr. Rick Florek of the Combined Arms Support Command's (CASCOM) Combat Service Support Battlelab; COL Kone Brugh, Deputy Commandant of the Ordnance Center and School; and COL Steven Bourgeois, Director of Combat Developments, Ordnance. A CSS Battlelab Army Transformation Wargame Combat Service Support Workshop was invaluable in helping me gain a background in Objective Force concepts.

The Honorable Eric Orsini, Deputy to the ASA(ALT) for Logistics, sponsored the research to other senior staff of the Office of the ASA(ALT) with the assistance of COL Glenn Harold. General (ret.) Leon Salomon engaged in several valuable discussions and provided insight into the Army Science Board's 2000 Summer Study with regard to reliability and maintainability issues. At the U.S. Army Evaluation Center (AEC), Dr. James Streilein (Director), Mr. Frank Apicella (Technical Director), Mr. Thomas Zeberlein, Mr. Freddie Player, Mr. Steve Yuhas, and LTC Cleon Raynor provided valuable insight into the role of requirements in terms of the evaluation process and prompted a critical examination of how combat damage should be treated in the development of equipment sustainment requirements. The AEC briefing has also led to a developing, collaborative effort to assess implementation requirements. Dr. David Mortin and Dr. Michael Cushing at the U.S. Army Materiel Systems Analysis Activity provided valuable information about similar, ongoing initiatives taking place in the Army, coordinated the AEC briefing, and have engaged in several thought-provoking discussions.

A series of senior-level briefings produced several improvements to the messages and the conclusions. Mr. Thomas Edwards, Deputy to the Commanding General of CASCOM, emphasized the need for the time-phased approach to requirements developed in the document and helped strengthen the discussion of this material. MG Mitchell

Stevenson, the Army's Chief of Ordnance, suggested the current introduction to the report, which motivates the need to improve Army equipment sustainment capabilities. LTG Mahan challenged us to further examine pulse availability and determine what the Army would have to do to improve the practicality of using this critical metric in the requirements and acquisition processes. This has spurred us to initiate a potentially valuable initiative to better incorporate equipment sustainment into combat modeling and to better understand the tradeoffs between better sustainment capability and other performance metrics. MG Robert Armbruster, Deputy for Systems Management and Horizontal Technology Integration, has pushed us to take the next steps and do the research necessary to take the conclusions from theory to practice.

At RAND, John Dumond, Director of the Arroyo Center's Military Logistics Program, has provided extensive recommendations and assistance with numerous iterations of the report as well as being always available to discuss ideas. He has also played an essential role in ensuring that the research directly addresses issues of importance to senior Army leaders. Rick Eden helped make major improvements to the report, especially with regard to the clarity of the message. His challenging questions with regard to many basic assumptions were frequently thought-provoking and led to new ideas and better support for arguments. Tom McNaugher also commented on draft briefings, thoroughly reviewed an earlier version of this document, provided valuable, detailed comments, and provided insight from his earlier research on DoD and Army weapon system development and acquisition—in particular, his detailed review of the program that resulted in the UH-60 Black Hawk. Kristin Leuschner did a great job boiling down the document to its essentials for the summary, and Jerry Sollinger helped clarify the language and better connect the chapters and concepts. John Matsumura and Jeff Drezner conducted thorough reviews that helped sharpen the discussion and ensure consistency throughout the report. Thanks go to Pamela Thompson for formatting and preparing the document and to Nikki Shacklett for her skillful editing.

ABBREVIATIONS

ACAT	Acquisition Category
AEC	U.S. Army Evaluation Center
ALDT	Administrative and Logistics Delay Time
AMSAA	Army Materiel Systems Analysis Activity
A_o	Operational Availability
AOE	Army of Excellence
APB	Acquisition Program Baseline
AROC	Army Requirements Oversight Council
ASA(ALT)	Assistant Secretary of the Army for Acquisition, Logistics, and Technology
ASL	Authorized Stockage List
AWCF	Army Working Capital Fund
AWP	Awaiting Parts
BCT	Brigade Combat Team
C4ISR	Command, Control, Communications, Computers, Intelligence, Surveillance, and Reconnaissance
CAE	Component Acquisition Executive
CDE	Combat Developments Engineering

CG	Commanding General
Class IX	Repair parts and components required for maintenance support of all equipment
CMFSV	Close Missile Fire Support Vehicle
CONUS	Continental United States
CSA	Chief of Staff of the Army
CSS	Combat Service Support
CSSC	Combat Service Support Company
CWT	Customer Wait Time
DCSOPS	Deputy Chief of Staff for Operations and Plans
DMDC	Defense Manpower Data Center
DoD	Department of Defense
DoDI	Department of Defense Instruction
DS	Direct Support
E-FOGM	Enhanced Fiber Optic Guided Missile
EDA	Equipment Downtime Analyzer
EFF	Essential Function Failure
ES	Equipment Sustainment
ESV	Engineer Support Vehicle
FAR	False Alarm Rate
FCS	Future Combat Systems
FEDC	Field Exercise Data Collection
FFD	Fraction of Faults Detected
FFP	Fraction of Faults Predicted
FFSD	Fraction of Faults Successfully Diagnosed
FFSP	Fraction of Faults Successfully Predicted
FIR	Fault Isolation Ratio (Isolation to One LRU/SRU)

FISO	Force Integration Staff Officer
FM	Force Management
FMC	Fully Mission Capable
FMECA	Failure Mode Effects and Criticality Analysis
FOV	Family of Vehicles
FY	Fiscal Year
GS	General Support
IAV	Interim Armored Vehicle
IBCT	Interim Brigade Combat Team
ICV	Infantry Carrier Vehicle
IDIV	Interim Division
ILAP	Integrated Logistics Analysis Program
IM	Item Manager
JCS	Joint Chiefs of Staff
JTR	Joint Transport Rotorcraft
KE	Kinetic Energy
KPP	Key Performance Parameter
LP CWT	Last Part Customer Wait Time
MaxTTR	Maximum Time to Repair
MBT	Main Battle Tank
MDTcd	Mean Downtime Per Combat Damage Event
MDTp	Mean Downtime Per Failure
MGS	Medium Gun System
MMBF	Mean Miles Between Failures
MMH	Maintenance Man-Hours
MOS	Military Occupational Specialty
MR	Maintenance Ratio

MTBCCD	Mean Time Between Critical Combat Damage
MTBCF	Mean Time Between Critical Failures
MTBEFF	Mean Time Between Essential Function Failures
MTBF	Mean Time Between Failures
MTBM	Mean Time Between Maintenance Actions
MTBSA	Mean Time Between System Aborts
MTBSM	Mean Time Between Scheduled Maintenance Actions
MTBUM	Mean Time Between Unscheduled Maintenance Actions
MTTR	Mean Time To Repair
MTTRp	Mean Time to Repair per Failure
NLOS	Non-Line of Sight
NMC	Not Mission Capable
NTC	National Training Center
O&M	Operations and Maintenance
O&S	Operating and Support
OIPT	Overarching Integrated Product Team
OMS/MP	Operational Mode Summary/Mission Profile
OP	Operational Profile
ORD	Operational Requirements Document
Org.	Organizational Maintenance
OTOE	Objective Table of Organization and Equipment
PLL	Prescribed Load List
PoF	Physics of Failure
RR	Remove and Replace
SAMS	Standard Army Maintenance System

SAR	Selected Acquisition Report
SDC	Sample Data Collection
SMA	Scheduled Maintenance Actions
SSA	Supply Support Activity
STX	Situational Training Exercise
TAADS	The Army Authorization Documents System
TRADOC	Training and Doctrine Command
TTHS	Transient, Trainee, Holdee, and Student
UAV	Unmanned Aerial Vehicle
ULLS	Unit Level Logistics System
UMA	Unscheduled Maintenance Actions
USC	United States Code
USD(AT&L)	Under Secretary of Defense (Acquisition, Technology, and Logistics)
VCSA	Vice Chief of Staff of the Army
WBO	Wholesale Backorder
WNBO	Wholesale Nonbackorder

Chapter One

DEFINING EQUIPMENT SUSTAINMENT REQUIREMENTS TO SUPPORT THE U.S. ARMY'S TRANSFORMATION

BACKGROUND

A central goal of the Army Transformation is to reduce the bulk or "footprint" of maneuver forces in order to increase deployment speed. Further, the Army is striving to reduce the relative size of combat service support (CSS) functions within a maneuver force: the maneuver force CSS footprint. The smaller the proportion of lift that has to be devoted to CSS equipment and supplies, the greater the proportion that can be devoted to moving weapon systems, thereby increasing the rate of combat power buildup.[1]

Emerging Objective Force operational concepts that envision a fast-paced, nonlinear battlefield with forces rapidly shifting across very large distances strengthen the need to achieve this footprint reduction goal—to enhance not only strategic but also operational and tactical mobility. Relatively "light" but powerful forces can take advantage of vertical mobility to gain operational freedom within a theater, and such forces would be less encumbered for high-speed ground movement. In addition, these operational concepts demand that maneuver forces be self-sustainable for short periods (e.g., three days) of intense operations—or what are being called combat or operational pulses—to create freedom of movement "untethered" from the need for secure lines of communication. Thus, CSS footprint in a maneuver force must be smaller, and, at the same time, the sustainment capability must be greater.[2]

---

[1]CSS footprint goals are found in "The Army's CS/CSS Transformation: Executive Summary," Briefing, January 21, 2000.

[2]For a discussion of future Army warfighting concepts and force requirements, see "Concepts for the Objective Force," United States Army White Paper, 2001.

Improving equipment sustainability is vital if the Army is to achieve dramatic CSS footprint reductions while maintaining or even improving the operational availability of its equipment, especially during operational pulses without external support. Equipment sustainability is defined as the Army's ability to keep equipment operational. This report focuses solely on the maintenance aspect of equipment sustainability, that is, whether equipment can be kept in proper working order. Two factors drive equipment sustainability: equipment supportability and logistics system capabilities. Supportability, which is a characteristic of weapon systems that can be influenced to the greatest degree in early design stages, is a measure of the amount and nature of resources needed to support a weapon system—in other words, how difficult and costly a system is to support. It is a function of reliability, maintainability, and durability. How many spare parts does it consume? What is the cost of these parts? How easy is to replace parts? Is special equipment needed to conduct maintenance? How much training is needed to diagnose faults? How frequently must a system be overhauled to stay in satisfactory condition? And so on. Logistics system capabilities are driven by supply, distribution, maintenance, and fleet life cycle management policies, processes, and resources. To the extent that requirements for these capabilities are specific to a weapon system program, they should be determined in conjunction with supportability requirements.

In addition to the need for better equipment sustainability, the emerging operational concepts that demand operational pulse self-sufficiency place new constraints on how forces can be sustained. As a result, the Army recognizes that business as usual will not suffice to develop the Objective Force's sustainability, in terms of both logistics concepts and capabilities and equipment supportability. Rather, innovative concepts of operations for logistics will probably have to be developed along with substantial design improvements for enhanced supportability. Advances on both fronts will be necessary to produce revolutionary levels of equipment sustainability achieved with minimal maintenance footprint (a subset of CSS footprint) in maneuver units.

When a new mission need is developed, the Army creates a mission need statement. If a materiel solution is deemed necessary to satisfy the mission need, then the Army's Training and Doctrine Command

(TRADOC), in conjunction with participants from many other Army organizations, develops the requirements (the capabilities that a system must have) deemed necessary to fulfill the mission need. Draft requirements may help guide concept development, and the final requirements serve as the basis for contractual specifications. Thus, these requirements play a key role in shaping the development of new weapon systems.

To communicate these requirements precisely, metrics must be employed. They enable the communication of precise target values for required capabilities, the development of a common understanding of the exact capability being sought, and the ability to measure whether a capability meets the needed level of performance. Thus it is critical for metrics to be aligned with requirements. That is, does a metric properly reflect the desired capability and drive design in the right direction? If the metric shows improvement, will the actual, physical improvement and benefit be what is expected and desired? Therefore, the development and use of good metrics is an integral part of the requirements development process.

As part of the process, a small number of the requirements may be designated as key performance parameters (KPPs). These are the absolutely essential operational capabilities that are deemed to form the basis of a system's value. In some sense, one might think of KPPs as representing the minimum essential set of capabilities that make a system worth buying. Other capabilities or higher levels of capabilities might increase mission performance or provide additional benefits and value, but the system might still have sufficient unique value with regard to the mission to make it worth buying even if it does not meet all of these "requirements." The Department of Defense (DoD) employs KPPs as a management tool to ensure the successful development of weapon systems. The way in which KPPs should be employed, by DoD policy, is described later in this report.

PURPOSE OF THIS REPORT

If business as usual will not suffice, then the question naturally arises as to whether the Army has been using the right equipment sustainment requirements and associated metrics, as well as the right KPPs, to achieve the desired equipment sustainability improvement. To help answer this question, the Assistant Secretary of the Army for

Acquisition, Logistics, and Technology (ASA[ALT]) asked RAND Arroyo Center to review current and proposed equipment sustainment requirements and their associated metrics, develop a recommended set of sustainment requirements and associated metrics for use in major acquisition programs, and assess the potential merit of these requirements as KPPs.

Setting good requirements is only one piece in the puzzle of how to improve equipment sustainability. In fact, the request to examine the potential merit of equipment sustainment requirements as KPPs was driven by a widespread belief that sustainment requirements are often traded off for other performance characteristics. Many in the Army's CSS community have realized that the Objective Force goals and the Army Transformation cannot be achieved if future equipment sustainment requirements are not generally satisfied. Thus, the Army must also develop better means to manage programs to preserve the necessary sustainability requirements as well as ensure that development efforts are sufficiently focused on improving the feasible levels of each equipment sustainment level, such as reliability and maintainability. This report focuses solely on developing good equipment sustainment requirements. However, the Army has several organizations and teams working on the improvement of program management targeted at achieving better equipment sustainability as well as programs to develop improved equipment sustainment capabilities through new technologies and concepts.

HOW THIS REPORT IS ORGANIZED

There are seven chapters in this report. Chapter Two motivates the importance of improving weapon system sustainability through a discussion of the three primary costs of poor sustainability: low mission or pulse availability, heavy maintenance footprint, and high cost. Chapter Three describes a framework for developing equipment sustainment requirements and metrics and presents a complete spectrum of requirements and metrics that should be considered when defining equipment sustainment requirements. Chapter Four briefly examines the data and methods necessary for effective use of this identified set of metrics and requirements. Chapter Five begins with a review of DoD and Army policy with regard to KPPs. The remainder of the chapter then reviews the recommended requirements in light of KPP policy in order to evaluate the potential merit of equipment sustainment requirements as KPPs. Chapter Six further illustrates some of the concepts discussed in the middle three chapters through a discussion of equipment sustainment requirements for the Future Combat Systems (FCS), the combat system that will be the heart of the Army's Objective Force. Chapter Seven provides a summary of conclusions and recommendations.

Chapter Two

THE COSTS OF POOR SUSTAINABILITY

Poor sustainability imposes substantial costs; this chapter details the most significant ones—not all of which are financial. One cost of poor sustainability is that equipment is not available to the desired degree to carry out a unit's mission. A second is that it leads to the need for a large maintenance footprint. This includes maintenance personnel (in lieu of "fighters") or additional lift to move a unit to and within a combat zone. The third major cost is, indeed, dollars: the money needed to maintain the Army's equipment.

THE FIRST COST: HIGH NMC RATE SPIKES AND LOW PULSE AVAILABILITY

The first critical "cost" of poor sustainability is low mission availability. However, this cost is often masked by current Army equipment readiness reporting, which averages the fully mission capable rate from the 16th of one month to the 15th of the next. When rolled up at the division level or higher for critical combat systems, these rates tend to meet or exceed the Army goals of 90 percent for ground systems and 75 percent for aviation. In Figure 2.1, the light gray horizontal lines near the 10 percent line depict such monthly averages for the M1A2 tanks in a heavy division.[1]

---

[1]The source of this data is the Equipment Downtime Analyzer (EDA), an information system tool developed at RAND and recently implemented by the Army in the Integrated Logistics Analysis Program that facilitates the diagnosis of equipment readiness. The EDA contains an archive of individual end item failures and downtime by day, which were aggregated to create this graph. The unit provided the training schedule superimposed on the graph. See Eric L. Peltz, Marc L. Robbins, Patricia

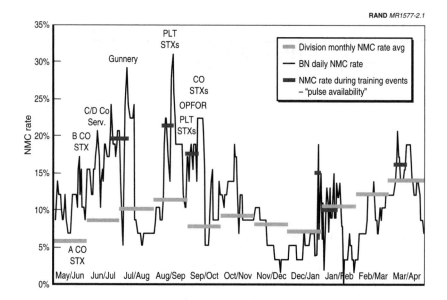

Figure 2.1—Monthly M1A2 NMC Rates for a Division and One of Its Battalions and Daily M1A2 NMC Rates for the Battalion

But behind these averages (the division average is a weighted average of the not-mission-capable (NMC) rates of its component battalions) of averages (each battalion's NMC rate is averaged over monthly periods), a different story unfolds.

The use of Army equipment is characterized by periods of inactivity with the equipment sitting idle in the motor pool, punctuated by relatively short periods of intense use during training exercises. Usually within a division, only some portion of the battalions are actively training in the field during any given month, and even those that are actively training have a combination of motor pool time and field exercise time. Within a battalion, equipment usage, in particular for primary weapon systems such as tanks, varies tremendously by day over the course of a year. Thus, most of the variation seen in

Boren, and Melvin Wolff, *Diagnosing the Army's Equipment Readiness: The Equipment Downtime Analyzer,* Santa Monica, CA: RAND, MR-1481-A, 2002, for a more complete discussion.

the jagged black line, which shows the daily NMC rate for the M1A2s of one armor battalion (in the same division as that depicted by the gray lines) over the course of one year, results from variation in the operating tempo. On average the availability often looks acceptable, but the average is merely a combination of low availability during periods of use and high availability during periods of inactivity. Therefore, average availability often does not reflect wartime equipment sustainment capability.

When focusing on actual daily NMC rates during battalion-level training exercises, we see that frequent and severe NMC rate peaks above 20 percent are common (e.g., during situational training exercises (STX)), and rates as high as 45 percent have been observed for M1A1 Abrams tanks as well as for many other types of equipment.[2] The average or "pulse availabilities" over the courses of training events often range from 15 to 25 percent. The short, black, horizontal lines depict the battalion's M1A2 pulse availability during training events (only those events in which the entire battalion participated).

THE SECOND COST: LARGE MAINTENANCE FOOTPRINT

Equipment reliability, combined with its maintainability and the support concepts employed, determines the necessary maintenance footprint to sustain a combat force at a given level of effectiveness. Figure 2.2 shows the relative sizes of the maintenance footprint across a range of division (DIV) and brigade combat team (BCT) types.[3] The personnel within these organizations are classified by their military occupational specialty (MOS) into four categories: combat arms (combat), combat support (CS), maintenance (maint), and other CSS personnel besides maintenance. Today this footprint

---

[2]Note that the NMC rates are solely a function of equipment failure. Combat damage could further increase the NMC rates.

[3]In the figure, AOE is an Army of Excellence unit, which is the name of the current organizational design basis for the Army's mechanized infantry and armor divisions. XXI is the Force XXI organizational design, which reorganized the AOE heavy division to take advantage of new information system capabilities and "digitized" equipment. LI DIV and LT INF (BCT) represent the Army's basic light infantry design. IDIV depicts the draft design of the Interim Division. SBCT is the new Stryker Brigade Combat Team, and the combat service support company (CSSC) is a planned SBCT augmentation element.

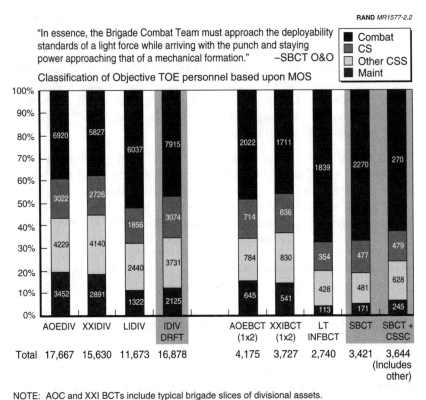

RAND MR1577-2.2

"In essence, the Brigade Combat Team must approach the deployability standards of a light force while arriving with the punch and staying power approaching that of a mechanical formation."   —SBCT O&O

Classification of Objective TOE personnel based upon MOS

- ■ Combat
- ■ CS
- □ Other CSS
- ■ Maint

	AOEDIV	XXIDIV	LIDIV	IDIV DRFT	AOEBCT (1x2)	XXIBCT (1x2)	LT INFBCT	SBCT	SBCT + CSSC
Total	17,667	15,630	11,673	16,878	4,175	3,727	2,740	3,421	3,644 (Includes other)

NOTE: AOC and XXI BCTs include typical brigade slices of divisional assets.

DATA SOURCE: Table of Organization and Equipment (TOE) database, provided by the U.S. Army Force Management Support Agency (USAFMSA).

Figure 2.2—The Relative Proportions of Personnel Categories Among Divisions and BCTs

is considered quite large—close to 20 percent of the personnel in both Army of Excellence (AOE) and Force XXI (XXI) heavy divisions are maintainers, and within these divisions about 15 percent of the personnel in task organized BCTs (with slices of divisional assets) are maintainers.[4] In addition, supply and transportation personnel

---

[4]The data in the figure were produced by categorizing the personnel in the Objective Tables of Organization and Equipment (OTOE) for each unit type by their military occupational specialties. Appendix B maps MOSs to categories.

provide spare parts to the maintainers and support the maintainers and their vehicles. The need for such a large maintenance footprint in the Army's combat organizations and the large supporting maintenance infrastructure in higher echelons is the second "cost" of poor sustainability.

As part of the Army Transformation, the Army intends to rely on substantially fewer maintainers to maintain the equipment in the Interim Division (draft) (IDIV) and the Stryker Brigade Combat Team (SBCT)—at least during combat pulses.[5] The ratio of maintainers to total personnel in the IDIV draft Objective Table of Organization and Equipment (OTOE) is almost half what it is in current heavy divisions, and the relative number of maintainers in the SBCT is about one-third that of a heavy brigade combat team. The percentage of SBCT personnel that are maintainers is still more than 50 percent lower than in current heavy brigade combat teams, even when the combat service company (CSSC) augments the SBCT. Both the IDIV's and the SBCT's mixes of personnel are remarkably similar to the distribution of personnel among MOSs in light divisions (LI DIV) and BCT (LI BCT). This is true despite the fact that these new organizations have substantially greater amounts of equipment than light infantry units.

For Objective Force units, the Army aims to reduce maintenance footprint (and other CSS elements) within maneuver forces to an even greater degree, with draft unit designs having a ratio of total personnel to maintainers two or more times higher than the SBCT's ratio. For the Interim and Objective Forces to be able to maintain equipment at a high level of operational availability, their equipment must have significantly better reliability and maintainability than that of current heavy units, logistics system capabilities must be much better, or there must be significant changes in support con-

---

[5]The current SBCTs are relying on augmentation from the CSSC, installation maintenance activities, and contractors to sustain their equipment in garrison. In a deployed environment, they will require the CSSC within a short time or in a high operating tempo situation; for extended operations, additional augmentation will be necessary for scheduled services.

cepts that leverage reach; more likely, success will take a combination of all three.[6]

THE THIRD COST: THE FINANCIAL COST OF MAINTAINING THE ARMY'S EQUIPMENT

The direct costs of maintaining the Army's equipment—paying maintenance and spare parts supply personnel, providing spare parts, paying for contract maintenance, and paying the personnel necessary to manage the maintenance system—accounted for about $8.5 billion, or more than 12 percent of the Army budget in 1999, which is the third cost of poor sustainability. Beyond the direct costs that could be isolated, additional indirect costs are associated with training (some training is included because maintenance personnel in instructor positions are included), maintenance infrastructure development and sustainment, policy analysis and management, a small number of transportation personnel driven by spare parts distribution requirements, recruiting, personnel management, and other overhead burdens. While the estimated cost may be less than some might have expected, it nevertheless represents a significant portion of the Army budget, and small decreases, say on the order of 10 percent, could make a real difference in the Army's ability to field new systems.

The pie chart in Figure 2.3 shows the relative contributions of the direct maintenance cost categories, while the bar graph more clearly shows the absolute sizes of each of these categories. The piece of the direct maintenance cost "pie" that usually garners the most attention is net operations and maintenance (O&M) spending on spare parts to the Army Working Capital Fund (AWCF), which covers all costs necessary to provide the spare parts needed by repair activities. Included in these costs are Army Materiel Command depot maintenance labor to repair reparable parts, procurement of consumable parts, procurement of repair parts to repair reparables, transportation and distribution, warehouse operations, supply management,

---

[6]Reach is defined as depending upon external resources for service or support. Reach could be to an intermediate support or staging base, a continental United States (CONUS) maintenance depot, a contractor in CONUS, a contractor in theater, a unit in CONUS, or any other externally located and nonorganic resource.

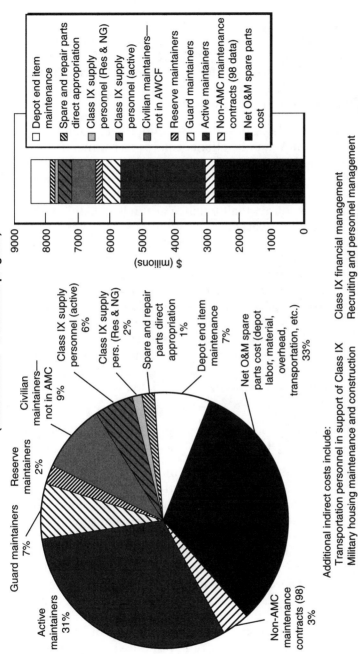

1999 Estimated Budget Costs Directly Related to Maintaining Army Equipment
(Initial estimate—work still in progress)

Legend:
- Depot end item maintenance
- Spare and repair parts direct appropriation
- Class IX supply personnel (Res & NG)
- Class IX supply personnel (active)
- Civilian maintainers— not in AWCF
- Reserve maintainers
- Guard maintainers
- Active maintainers
- Non-AMC maintenance contracts (98 data)
- Net O&M spare parts cost

$ (millions): 9000, 8000, 7000, 6000, 5000, 4000, 3000, 2000, 1000, 0

Pie chart labels:
- Civilian maintainers— not in AMC 9%
- Class IX supply personnel (active) 6%
- Class IX supply pers. (Res & NG) 2%
- Spare and repair parts direct appropriation 1%
- Depot end item maintenance 7%
- Reserve maintainers 2%
- Guard maintainers 7%
- Active maintainers 31%
- Non-AMC maintenance contracts (98) 3%
- Net O&M spare parts cost (depot labor, material, overhead, transportation, etc.) 33%

Additional indirect costs include:
Transportation personnel in support of Class IX   Class IX financial management
Military housing maintenance and construction   Recruiting and personnel management
Facilities maintenance and construction   Support of Class IX and maintenance operations
Development and testing

Figure 2.3—The Direct Costs of Maintaining the Army's Equipment by Category

overall management, and other overhead expenses. Note that although it is large, spare parts spending accounts for only one-third of equipment maintenance costs. Outside of the AWCF, the Army Materiel Command spends money for end item overhauls. Thus in 1999, 40 percent of the Army's maintenance spending was for Army wholesale supply and maintenance activities.

The total spending (pay and benefits) for Army military maintainers—active, Army Reserve, and National Guard—accounted for another 40 percent. Adding in Army civilian maintainers not in repair depots brought the non-depot-maintenance labor bill close to 50 percent of maintenance expenditures. The final portion of spending on "maintainers" is contract maintenance at the installation level. (Recently, some civilian maintenance operations have been contracted out, which could have affected the mix between contract maintenance and civilian maintainers.) "Maintainers" is in quotation marks because some of these contracts cover all costs of maintenance, including labor and spare parts. The next major piece is Class IX (spare parts) supply personnel who run Class IX supply support activities (SSA) and operate the Unit Level Logistics System (ULLS) and Standard Army Maintenance System (SAMS) computers in Army maintenance shops that are used to manage maintenance and order parts. The final piece is the direct appropriation of funds for spare and repair parts procurement associated with new equipment fielding.

Appendix C provides the sources, assumptions, and calculations used to develop the estimates for each category.

To put direct maintenance expenditures in perspective, Figure 2.4 compares the direct maintenance costs with the total Army budget by major budget category. The estimate of total direct spending on maintenance in 1999 represents more than 12 percent of the Army budget. Most of this money is spent through the O&M and military personnel accounts, with a small portion coming through procurement. O&M expenses include spare parts (which includes civilian labor, purchases of spare and repair parts, transportation, etc.), depot end item maintenance (includes civilian labor, purchases of spare and repair parts, etc.), Army civilian maintainers, and maintenance contracts. Funds for the initial provisioning of spare and repair parts for new weapon systems, or in response to other needed

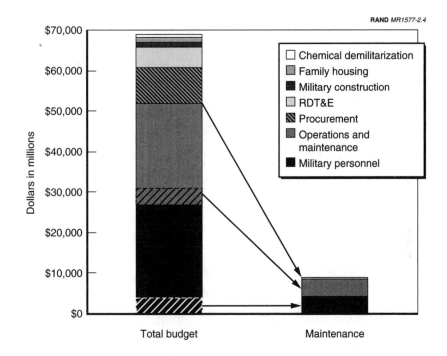

Figure 2.4—Direct Maintenance Costs by Budget Account

changes in inventory (e.g., end item modifications), are provided
through the procurement budget.

Chapter Three

HOW SHOULD EQUIPMENT SUSTAINMENT REQUIREMENTS BE DEFINED AND MEASURED?

The previous chapter described the three costs of poor sustainability. This chapter turns to a discussion of how to define requirements to improve the sustainability of future equipment. It recommends high-level equipment sustainment goals and describes how these goals should factor into the requirements and acquisition processes. Then it proposes a potential template of metrics to define and measure sustainment requirements that should be considered in all major end item acquisition programs. Finally, it examines a cross-section of Army requirements documents to assess the degree to which these requirements and metrics have been employed by the Army.

GENERAL EQUIPMENT SUSTAINMENT GOALS

The three costs reflect the three general primary reasons the Army cares about equipment sustainment. The Army wants equipment available for use when needed to accomplish missions; wants this equipment kept available with as small a maneuver force maintenance footprint as possible; and wants the maintenance of equipment to cost as little as possible. Each goal is directly affected through quantifiable relationships by the reliability and the maintainability (to include durability) of equipment; the fleet life cycle management effectiveness; the amount of supply chain and maintenance resources available; the effectiveness of the supply chain and maintenance processes; and the support concepts employed. These "levers" might be considered the inputs to equipment sustainability, with the goals representing the outputs, as depicted in Figure 3.1.

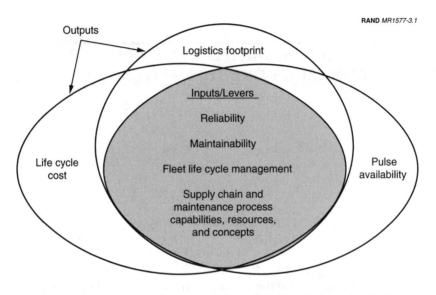

A change in any one of the inputs or "levers" is likely to impact multiple "outputs" or goals and not necessarily in the same direction

Figure 3.1—General Equipment Sustainment Levers and Goals

Depending upon the action, an improvement in one of these levers could positively affect all three higher-level goals, but at other times a change in one may result in tradeoffs among goals. For example, more maintainers might increase availability (depending upon whether capacity is constrained or not) but would add footprint and cost. While the focus sometimes becomes more intense on one of these levers, each can play a substantial role in helping the Army reach its ultimate sustainment goals.

Tailoring Equipment Sustainment Goals to the Army Transformation

When determining equipment sustainment requirements, the Army, as with all other requirements, should tailor these general goals in accordance with the overall operational goals and the concepts that have been identified as the best approaches for achieving them. The Army has articulated overall and operational goals and concepts for the Objective Force, as arrayed around the overlapping ovals in Figure 3.2. They describe concisely how the Army intends to structure and employ its force to fight in the 2025 time frame.

These operational goals and concepts have implications for logistics and readiness that the Army has also identified and that are described in outer portions of the four overlapping ovals in Figure 3.2. As discussed previously, the desire to have a rapidly deployable force drives the need to minimize the maintenance footprint that must be deployed, and the desire for extreme operational and tactical mobility over extreme distances further demands a low maintenance footprint in the maneuver force. Combining the extended operational distances envisioned with the desire to conduct nonlinear operations with forces widely distributed across a combat zone, which will produce noncontiguous lines of communication, generates the need for

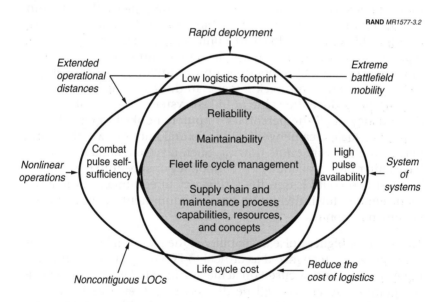

RAND *MR1577-3.2*

Objective Force and Transformation goals and concepts
Logistics and readiness implications → Overall equipment sustainment goals
"Levers" influencing each of the overall equipment sustainment goals

**Figure 3.2—Tailoring Equipment Sustainment Goals to the
Army Transformation**

maneuver force self-sufficiency during what is becoming known as combat pulses. A force will move out and conduct continuous operations without external support for a given period of time (for example, three days), before it comes back to some sort of base or "plugs in" to a support unit to prepare or "refit" for another pulse. As a result of new Objective Force concepts, self-sufficiency becomes a fourth overall equipment sustainment goal beyond the three general ones identified in Figure 3.1.

The Army has always been concerned with the need to have available equipment, but, as we will discuss in more detail later, the notion of an FCS as a system of systems with strong interdependencies—which introduces network availability issues to combat forces—potentially implies higher-than-ever equipment availability requirements at the system level, depending upon how the overall network is designed. For example, in a traditional armor company of 14 tanks, one might think of the loss of one tank as the loss of one-fourteenth of its combat power; the loss of a single tank has limited effect on the value of the other 13. Compare this with a unit composed of several different types of systems, some of which depend upon others, such as indirect-fire systems depending upon unmanned aerial vehicles (UAVs) to identify and track targets. In this case, the loss of a UAV can sharply reduce the value of linked systems. (This is akin to the dependency of all the personal computers hooked to each hub or router in a local area network. If the central hub is down, this entire part of the network shuts down.) Such a system should probably have either high availability or redundancy or substitutable "nodes." The last two could lessen the stringency of equipment availability requirements for individual pieces of equipment or even make a system more robust.

The need for higher pulse availability at the platform level is increasingly becoming recognized as critical to FCS development. Initially, the Army was more focused on achieving high or "ultra" reliability at the platform level. As will be discussed further, this is just one means, albeit an important one, of achieving high availability at the platform level, which is just one means of achieving high network availability.

Finally, the Army and DoD have been increasing the emphasis on the life cycle cost of programs over the last few years as they have come to understand that the bulk of life cycle cost comes not from acquisition, but from operating and support costs. By acquisition policy, life cycle cost must be tracked and targeted in all programs.

MEANS FOR ACHIEVING EQUIPMENT SUSTAINMENT GOALS

To support Army Transformation, within the categories presented in the middle of Figure 3.2, the CSS community has begun to determine the concepts to be employed and the principles to be followed in the creation of CSS structure, CSS doctrine, and equipment design to meet Army Transformation goals and to support Objective Force operational concepts.   For instance, through better reliability and maintainability (e.g., prognostic capabilities), the Army will be able to reduce critical failures during combat pulses both because there will be fewer failures and because it will be far better able to anticipate the remaining failures and replace soon-to-fail components before commencing operations.   Better maintainability can also reduce downtime and resource requirements when failures do occur, and it could facilitate the ability of operators and crews to take on greater maintenance responsibility, thereby reducing footprint. Increasing platform commonality can improve supply support for a given level of investment and footprint. Successfully employing these concepts and principles becomes the objective of CSS system and weapon system design. To the extent that weapon system design and program requirements can help achieve these objectives, they should be emphasized in operational requirements. Other objectives, such as those involving spare parts distribution, are broader in scope than any one program and will be driven primarily by efforts outside of weapon system procurement.

Consistent with the Objective Force–derived logistics and readiness goals, the Army has developed aggressive CSS Transformation goals with regard to increasing deployment speed, reducing CSS footprint, and reducing the cost of logistics. It has been recognized that these aggressive goals probably cannot be achieved solely through changes in logistics structure and processes. In conjunction with these changes, it is also essential to change radically the nature and number of demands that the Army's equipment places on the logistics system. Therefore, the acquisition process must play a key role in achieving not just Army Transformation and Objective Force operational goals, but also CSS Transformation goals.

Nothing that the Army is talking about with regard to improving equipment sustainability is fundamentally new from a functional design standpoint. Also not new is the ultimate purpose of equipment sustainment—the ability to provide and sustain combat power during operations—or the types of costs it imposes. What are new are the objectives for the overall requirements, which are unprecedented in their demands (due to unprecedented operational demands). What are also new are some of the assumed constraints (e.g., combat pulse self-sufficiency).

THE ROLES OF OVERALL GOALS AND FUNCTIONAL DESIGN REQUIREMENTS

In the framework just discussed, two types of equipment sustainment requirements begin to emerge for the development of the Army's Objective Force. The first type consists of overarching equipment sustainment goals driven by overall Army operational and cost goals that represent composite measures of logistics system and equipment design parameters. They are

- High pulse availability.

- Low maintenance footprint.

- Combat pulse self-sufficiency.

- Low life cycle equipment sustainment cost.

DoD acquisition policy has been increasing its emphasis on the use of broad goals such as these, because they allow flexibility in designing concepts, logistics processes, fleet management strategies, and equipment that will meet operational needs. In short, they enable effective use of tradeoffs. By providing the freedom to find the best way to improve performance, they foster innovation and empower suppliers by keeping options open.

However, performance against these overarching goals is often not measurable and is often beyond the scope of responsibility of one organization; rather, overarching measures of performance are functions of many design elements. Instead, one-dimensional, functional requirements that can be directly aligned with design characteristics and directly measured facilitate successful program management, which requires the achievement of a specified level of performance, on time, and within budget. Clear, precisely measurable metrics that are narrowly defined along functional lines allow performance feedback and accountability throughout a program. Their use enables program management to monitor performance along each design dimension before the full system has to come together. In addition, if a shortfall occurs with regard to an overarching goal, having measures for each of its component design characteristics will help isolate the source of the shortfall and facilitate the identification of ways to fix it.

The broad, overarching goals and the metrics selected to communicate performance against these goals should be oriented toward developing concepts and then selecting the preferred concept. Once the final concept is selected, detailed requirements can then be specified based on the conceptual design. The use of detailed requirements is necessary to ensure that the Army gets what it has been promised. However, if these detailed requirements are specified too soon in a new weapon system program, the Army runs the danger of prematurely eliminating a better overall solution set. *In other words, the selected concept represents a promise to achieve the overall goals based on a set of design assumptions. The role of the detailed requirements is to ensure that these assumptions are met so that the overall goals are achieved.* Thus, the two types of requirements are complementary. Each overarching goal is a composite one that is a function of several one-dimensional functional requirements and the environment in which the equipment will be employed (e.g., operating concepts and mission profiles).

The Evolution of Requirements

When an acquisition program starts, as long as there are competing concepts, it is undesirable to define the entire set of equipment sustainment requirements in precise detail, particularly those oriented to one-dimensional functional design objectives. Instead, during concept exploration, the Army should first assess how the mission need influences the importance of each of the overall equipment sustainment goals; it may become apparent that multiple goals, such as footprint and availability, have unusually high importance to a program. For example, an item that deploys forward should have a smaller local maintenance footprint in order to be mobile than one that operates from the rear. Or it could be determined that there is a hard constraint for one of the goals. For example, a deployment analysis might show that the maintenance footprint has to be less than or equal to some value. From this examination, high-level goals should be set in terms of availability, footprint, life cycle cost, and self-sufficiency. Understanding the balance needed in a program as well as the desire for the absolute levels of each goal should then drive the means, in other words the design features, that receive the most emphasis as contractors perform concept and technology development.

As concept and technology development and assessments evolve, the program and each concept team should start generating estimates of feasible ranges of reliability and maintainability and the risks associated with relying on various levels of performance along these and other dimensions. Based on these estimates, the program can assess the feasible levels of each overall goal that could reasonably be achieved through different combinations of reliability, maintainability, fleet life cycle management plans, and supply chain support. Each estimated potential level for an overall goal would carry a level of risk derived from the risks associated with achieving the related, functional design objectives. Each such combination of levels of the functional design objectives comprises an alternative concept, as illustrated by the three concepts on the left side of Figure 3.3. Finally, through joint consideration of the overall goals, the Army has to compare the overall value and risk of each concept and then decide which to pursue.

Once a concept is selected, typically at Milestone B of the acquisition process, the design assumptions upon which the expected performance of this concept rest should become the detailed program requirements, as seen in the figure. At this point, the requirements should be fully specified for Operational Requirements Document (ORD) validation. In cases where the Army or DoD elects to continue competition past Milestone B through multiple development efforts, then the detailed requirements derivation should be delayed until the program selects one concept.

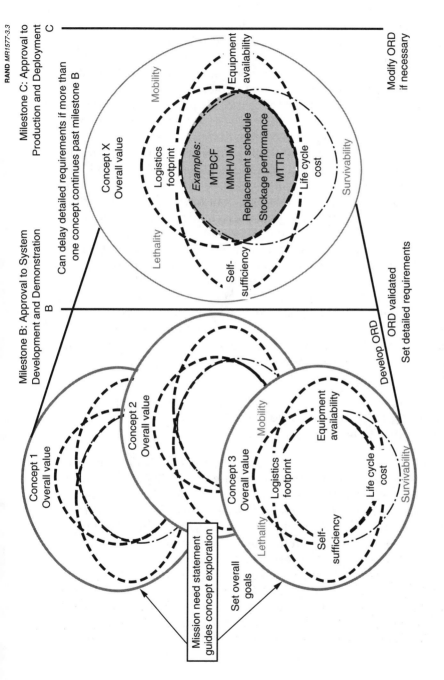

Figure 3.3—The Evolution of Program Requirements

As concept and technology development progresses, a broad tradespace bounded and guided by the mission need statement should gradually narrow until it collapses on a solution set when one concept is selected. In the first iteration of requirements determination for inclusion in an initial ORD, targets for each of the overall goals should be determined. These include pulse operational availability, life cycle cost, self-sufficiency (if applicable), and maintenance footprint. Concept exploration determines the best way (i.e., mix of reliability and maintainability initiatives, supply chain support, life cycle planning, etc.) to achieve these objectives, and then the resulting solution set becomes the operational requirements in the validated ORD. The large trades will have been made by this point, and the "official" tradespace exists between the threshold and objective for each requirement. An unofficial tradespace, though, extends beyond the thresholds for non-KPP requirements. (Chapter Five's discussion of KPPs compares the "power" of thresholds for KPP and non-KPP designated requirements.) Tradeoffs beyond the thresholds are likely to be "negative" in nature, barring unexpected technological breakthroughs. For example, it may be found to be infeasible to achieve the reliability target. Then a decision has to be made with regard to either relaxing the pulse operational availability (A_o) requirement or achieving it by adding more logistics resources, which would increase footprint and cost.

Program and Contract Scope Considerations Drive the Need for Detailed Requirements

If a contract is to be sufficiently broad, then it may not be necessary to determine and specify detailed requirements. Rather, if contractors have a sufficiently broad scope of work in which they control all the necessary levers, they could retain flexibility to find the best way to meet the overall goals throughout the program. There has probably not been any program in the past for which this approach would have been applicable. However, there seems to be increasing discussion of innovative approaches to weapon system contracting, such as buying "power by the hour" or even lease-use agreements, which would imply a broad scope of contractor logistics support. Such programs could simply specify, for example, an availability-oriented requirement, a deployed maintenance footprint requirement, and cost requirements (as well as pulse self-sufficiency as applicable).

When a program scope encompasses the responsibility of more than one organization, as they typically do, then the detailed, functional requirements are necessary to align requirements with each organization's scope of responsibility. The program should still retain the overall requirements. It becomes the program responsibility to manage these by ensuring that the responsible organizations all meet their functional requirements and leveraging the tradespace when shortfalls do occur. For instance, reliability and maintainability would usually be within the scope of a weapon system contractor, while spare parts provisioning and overhaul/recapitalization planning would be the responsibility of the Army. Achieving or resourcing all of these requirements would be necessary to reach the pulse A_o requirement, but this is a program requirement, and not the responsibility of either the contractor or the organizations that provide spare parts and overhaul.

Time-Phased, Evolutionary Requirements

During concept exploration, it may be determined that emerging technologies or other concepts could lead to better performance but that they will not be mature by the desired initial fielding date. Or in today's climate of rapidly advancing technology, new developments may materialize after the ORD is finalized. Such capabilities may be targeted for inclusion in subsequent fielding blocks to achieve a full operational capability in the time-phased approach advocated by DoD acquisition policy. This time-phased approach enables more evolutionary or iterative development that prevents a weapon system from becoming locked into aging technology.

EQUIPMENT SUSTAINMENT REQUIREMENTS FOR THE ARMY

We now turn to how the overall and design equipment sustainment requirements should be defined and measured. The list of requirements in Tables 3.1 and 3.2 provides a recommended starting point for the development of a standard set of equipment sustainment requirements and associated metrics that all programs should con-

Table 3.1

Equipment Sustainment Overall Goals and Metrics

Requirement Category	Equipment Sustainment Program Goals	Potential Standard Metrics for Defining Sustainment Requirements
Availability	• Meet mission needs • Maximize pulse availability • Maximize sortie availability	• Pulse A_o (operational availability) — Use derived pulse A_i in some cases • Prob(successful sortie completion) • Specify pulse, refit, and sortie parameters[a]
Self-sufficiency	• Unit self-sufficiency during pulses	• Self-sufficiency pulse length
Equipment sustainment footprint	• Minimize deployment footprint and maneuver force footprint	• Maintainers by echelon (cost and footprint driver); may be relative or maintenance ratio by echelon • Maintenance equipment lift requirements
Life cycle equipment sustainment cost	• Minimize life cycle cost	• Total life cycle cost to "maintain" • Annual operation (cost per operating hour/mile) • Planned recapitalization • Spare parts provisioning • Investment in reliability (e.g., materiel)

[a]Critical assumptions that are necessary to determine the associated requirements.

sider for use. The list also notes certain critical assumptions for determining the thresholds and objectives for each requirement. Such a list could create common ground from which all Army materiel development proponents could work, and it would help align all programs with overall Army goals and equipment sustainment design trends. As methods for achieving the overall goals become identified as desired solutions, the Army can, where it makes sense, drive their adoption through consistent emphasis in new programs. For example, many have come to believe that a shift toward anticipa-

Table 3.2

Equipment Sustainment Functional Design Requirements and Metrics

Requirement Category	Equipment Sustainment Functional Design Objectives	Potential Standard Metrics for Defining Equipment Sustainment Requirements
Reliability	• Minimize mission-critical failures • Minimize maintenance requirements	• Standard form of MTBCF • MTBUM and MTBSM (by echelon)
Maintainability	• Prevent faults from becoming mission critical • Minimize downtime and cost • Minimize maintenance footprint and cost • Minimize maintenance footprint forward	• FFSP = Fn(FFP, FIR, FAR/NEOF Rate) • FFSD = Fn(FFD, FIR, FAR/NEOF Rate) • MTTR (by echelon) • MMH/UM (by echelon) • MMH/SM (by echelon) • Percent UM-crew, org, DS, GS
Fleet life cycle management	• Recognize life cycle costs up front • Account for life cycle operations • Sustain reliability and maintainability at necessary levels	• Specify replacement/recap/overhaul retirement schedule and methods • Use estimate of reliability degradation in requirements analysis[a]
Supply support	• Minimize CWT • Minimize cost and footprint	• Local fill rate • Battle damage parts kit • Wholesale backorder rate • Percent of parts that are unique • Number and positioning of end item "spares" • Specify ALDT assumption[a]

[a]Critical assumptions that are necessary to determine the associated requirements.

tory maintenance enabled by prognostic capabilities is essential to achieve reduced maneuver force maintenance footprint yet still maintain a high level of equipment availability. If prognostics or any other design feature, such as automated diagnostics that enable increased crew maintenance, is truly an essential enabler of achieving transformation goals, then the Army should ensure that each program works toward achieving the needed capability. A standard set of requirements would be useful to the Army in its quest to transform and move toward radically new concepts for deployment and operations—concepts that require dramatic reductions in maintenance footprint while maintaining high levels of force capability.

Not all of the requirements apply to all programs. In general, the larger and more significant a program is to the Army's future, the more the program will be able to influence the entire spectrum of requirements, and thus it becomes more feasible to employ a broad spectrum of these requirements. At the other extreme, a nondevelopmental program will have very little influence over many of these requirements, and thus few will make sense for a program to use.

To develop this standard set of equipment sustainment requirements, we start with the overall equipment sustainment goals presented previously in Figure 3.2 that flow from overall operational objectives and concepts. In the list, we divide the equipment sustainment requirements into categories based on the overall goals and the various levers for achieving them. Then, for each category we list metrics that would effectively measure performance against desired capabilities. Table 3.1 describes requirements and metrics for the overall goals, and Table 3.2 lists the functional design requirements—root-level measures that together determine performance against the overall goals. These are requirements that product engineers and logistics system designers can directly affect. The next two sections of this chapter explain the requirements and metrics in detail, and Appendix F provides a metrics template guide to include definitions, important considerations, how each metric provides value, and assumptions.

OVERALL GOALS

Availability

To reflect the ability to keep equipment available for use during combat or other operations—the ultimate purpose of equipment sustainment—the use of the metric "pulse A_o" is suggested. Pulse A_o is defined in this document as the percentage of time a system is available over the course of a combat pulse, which is equivalent to the probability that the system is operational at any point in time during a pulse. An alternative form of a pulse A_o requirement would be to specify a probability of maintaining a minimum A_o over the course of an entire combat pulse for a unit—call this minimum pulse A_o. This would be important when a minimum level is deemed necessary to maintain a unit's combat effectiveness. Pulse A_o, in one or both of these forms, is what the operator cares about.

It is affected by the initial availability when the pulse starts, mission-critical failures that occur during the pulse, and the ability of the logistics system (including the crew) to return NMC items to mission-capable status during the pulse. In support of determining pulse A_o from functional design objectives such as reliability, the ORD should reference the pulse length, the operating profile, and the refit period from the operational mode summary/mission profile (OMS/MP).[1] Although minimizing cost and footprint are also overall goals, they can be thought of as the negative consequences of what it takes to keep equipment operational. Each functional design requirement is oriented to maximizing A_o while minimizing footprint and cost and maintaining pulse self-sufficiency.

Since pulse A_o is defined in terms of a combat pulse, it should not be affected by scheduled maintenance, which should be executed before operations or during refit periods, or noncritical maintenance actions, which can be deferred.[2] Thus, it can be defined as

$$\frac{MTBCF}{MTBCF + MDTp}$$

(assuming initial A_o is 100 percent), where *MTBCF* is the mean time between critical failures and *MDTp* is the mean downtime per failure during the combat pulse.[3] However, as we will discuss later, *MDTp*

---

[1] A refit period is a new concept being considered for the Objective Force sustainment concept in conjunction with operational pulses. Self-sufficient pulses would be followed by "refit" periods in which forces would rest, recover, and resupply to prepare for another pulse.

[2] Noncritical maintenance actions or faults are those that do not make the system unsafe to use and that do not affect mission capability, such as a bent fender or the first loss of a redundant set of parts that provide an essential capability.

[3] If a minimum pulse A_o requirement were used instead of an average pulse A_o, simulation rather than an equation would have to be used to determine the minimum

or the average total broke-to-fix time may be beyond the scope of the system developer's work. In cases where the developer is only responsible for designing the maintainability of the system to achieve a required mean time to repair (MTTR) rather than having the ability to affect the entire down time period,[4] the program could focus on pulse A_0 but from it derive a required pulse inherent availability, pulse A_i, defined as

$$\frac{MTBCF}{MTBCF + MTTRp},$$

where *MTTRp* is the MTTR for mission-critical failures during combat pulses. Or the program could still specify an A_0 but also specify the assumption for the administrative lead time (ALDT) during combat pulses, defined as *MDTp − MTTRp*. In either scenario, the program and internal DoD logistics providers would then be responsible for ensuring that the logistics system could meet the ALDT assumption. In cases with a very broad scope of work—in which the developer is responsible for spare parts planning or total logistics support as well as equipment design—then it could be reasonable to directly specify pulse A_0 as a requirement intended to become a contractual design specification.

The critical failures that ultimately drive pulse A_0 are not due to equipment breakdown or reliability alone; they may also include battle damage. However, the focus should initially be on ensuring that equipment supportability and logistics capability requirements are met—that these aspects of the design and development process are executed well. Thus the metrics used in the pulse A_0 equations in this section only reflect reliability failures, not combat damage. Later in the development process, operational evaluations can pull together survivability and equipment sustainability as part of the

---

pulse A_0 at a given level of confidence. Even with an average pulse A_0 requirement, though, the use of a simulation as described in the next chapter of this report and in Appendix A would be useful.

[4]MTTR is defined as the "clock" time it takes a repairer to diagnose faults and complete the repair, assuming all the necessary diagnostic equipment and parts are available. It is sometimes known as "wrench-turning time."

overall system and force effectiveness evaluations.[5] Sensitivity of the overall pulse A_o (including combat damage) to a range of combat damage assumptions can be explored to help assess the overall effectiveness. Such sensitivity analysis is necessary because combat damage varies greatly depending upon the specifics of the combat situation.

Another potential way to treat the issue of combat damage would be to provide a "cushion" for some level of anticipated combat damage when determining the required pulse A_o (without combat damage) targets. Alternatively, the full definition of A_o with combat damage could be employed in conjunction with an assumption for MTBCCD. Either route would produce more aggressive equipment sustainment requirements. However, given the uncertainty of combat damage rates, the meaningfulness of these approaches is likely to be low, and any derived requirements would be extraordinarily easy to challenge. Thus, the current Army practice of not including estimates of combat damage rates when determining A_o targets should continue.

Within the category of availability, the list in Table 3.1 includes one overall goal that has not been previously discussed—sortie reliability—which also relates directly to mission needs. Sortie reliability is the probability that an item will be able to execute an intended sortie or mission task (from a maintenance standpoint). Will a missile complete its flight without malfunctioning? Can a helicopter reach and attack a target without breaking down? Can a tank cross the line of departure and assault an enemy position without experiencing a critical operating failure? Sortie reliability becomes important when looking at a period in which reliability is the primary equipment

---

[5]When assessing overall pulse A_o, including equipment sustainability and survivability, a broader analysis of pulse A_o would incorporate combat damage and the definition would expand to $\dfrac{MTBCF + MTBCCD}{MTBCF + MDTp + MTBCCD + MDTcd}$ (assuming initial A_o is 100 percent), where $MTBCF$ is the mean time between critical failures, $MTBCCD$ is mean time between critical combat damage events, $MDTp$ is the mean downtime per failure during the combat pulse, and $MDTcd$ is the mean downtime per critical combat damage event during the pulse. $MTBCF$ and $MTBCCD$ can be combined in a metric called mean time between critical downing events. Once equipment sustainability is well understood, a range of assumptions with regard to combat damage can be applied to evaluate the ability of the system to cope with both equipment failure and combat damage.

sustainment factor that affects mission success. The determination of sortie reliability is based upon those failures that cannot be repaired in time to complete a sortie or mission task once it has been initiated. Thus, maintainability features that allow a system to continue on a mission without "losing stride" (e.g., resetting a computer after a software failure as a tank continues maneuvering with its platoon) can also affect sortie reliability. In other words, this metric is concerned with those failures for which there is absolutely no possibility of completing repair in time to affect sortie or mission task success. As inherent reliability decreases or this period increases, this metric becomes more important. If one were to conclude that absolutely no repair was possible during several consecutive sorties or tasks that occur over the course of a combat pulse, then one might think about pulse reliability or the probability that a system could complete a combat pulse without failure.

Sortie and pulse reliability are overall goals for two reasons: They directly interest the operator, and they are not metrics posed solely in equipment design terms. They are a function of five elements: MTBCF, the length of the sortie or pulse, the operating profile during the sortie or pulse, quick fault-correction capability, and the ability to anticipate and correct probable faults before the sortie or pulse. Of these five, MTBCF and the two maintainability elements (quick fault-correction capability and the ability to predict faults) are one-dimensional functional design requirements. The other two, sortie or pulse length and the operating profile, should be specified assumptions used to determine the sortie or pulse reliability requirement and should be referenced in the ORD. These profiles are currently provided in the OMS/MP.

Objective Force concepts envision combat pulses followed by refit periods during which units would prepare for another combat pulse. Refit activities could include deferred repair of failures or combat damage that occurred during pulses (though evacuation may not occur and supplies may not be shipped forward to maneuver forces during combat pulses, information about part and maintenance requirements should flow to the necessary providers to facilitate refit preparation), anticipatory maintenance based on predicted failures, scheduled services, and possibly some recovery of assets left behind on the battlefield. The length of the refit period will be an important parameter in determining the level of resources needed to conduct refit operations to produce a given level of availability heading into the next pulse. This affects the ability to maintain the desired level of pulse A_o over multiple pulses (which depends partly on successful accomplishment of anticipatory maintenance and services executed to standard). Rather than being a requirement, the refit length will be an assumption or input that will be a critical driver of other requirements. Thus, the assumption should be specified in the ORD to create a common understanding of what the requirements are based on and under what conditions they can reasonably be achieved.

Another critical assumption that has to be made is the degree to which broken or damaged end items will be recovered during combat pulses. What will happen to immobilized equipment that cannot be repaired by the maneuver force's organic maintenance capability? What will happen to immobilized equipment within the force's repair capability that cannot be repaired before the highly mobile force performs another extended maneuver? Will immobilized equipment be blown up in place? Will it be evacuated by like systems? If so, how will this affect combat power during pulses? Or will there be a handful of recovery vehicles? The answers to these questions could play a critical role in the benefits of refit and the type of work performed during refit. In the extreme case, refit could consist primarily of end item replacement, prognostic maintenance, services, and deferred maintenance on still-mobile equipment, with all immobilized equipment being left behind.

Self-sufficiency

In cases where it is desired that the pulse A_o be achieved without external support, self-sufficiency should be an overall goal. Self-sufficiency from a maintenance standpoint is defined as a period during which an organization will operate without any resupply of spare parts or maintenance support from units that are not part of the maneuver force. This also implies that there will not be any retrograde of broken components. The length of the period would be defined by the combat pulse length specified in the OMS/MP for the system. To achieve a desired level of A_o, self-sufficiency has implications for the required levels of reliability, maintainability, amount of spare parts, and maintenance capacity within the maneuver force.

Maintenance Footprint

From the pulse A_o requirement, refit assumptions, the self-sufficiency requirement, reliability requirements, combat damage rate assumptions, and maintainability requirements, the Army can determine the maintenance capacity in terms of personnel and equipment necessary at each echelon. Alternatively, these capacity requirements could be fixed if it is desired to constrain footprint to a certain level and then one would derive one or more of the other requirements. Two simple footprint metrics, the number of maintenance personnel and the lift requirements for equipment by echelon, should be sufficient. The number of personnel and the amount of equipment they have create demand for strategic lift, intratheater lift for nonlinear operations, and sustainment resources (water, food, fuel, food service personnel, medical personnel, force protection, etc.). An alternative metric for the personnel portion of footprint would be the maintenance ratio (MR) by echelon, where the maintenance ratio equals maintenance hours divided by operating hours. MR keeps operating hours as a variable, whereas the other two metrics require it to be fixed (i.e., use of a pulse operating hour assumption). To focus development efforts, separate metrics should track maintenance footprint requirements driven by equipment failure and those driven by combat damage.

Cost

Total life cycle cost related to equipment sustainment should include annual maintenance support costs, initial spare parts provisioning, and any planned recapitalization or overhaul costs. Support cost could be measured in terms of support cost per operating mile (hour), per round expended, or any other usage characteristic that drives the maintenance requirement for an end item. Equipment sustainment life cycle costs could also include design-driven costs where design decisions made solely to improve reliability or maintainability increase cost. This could include component or subsystem redundancy, more robust components, failure-prevention sensors, new materials, and built-in prognostic or diagnostic sensors and automation.

EQUIPMENT SUSTAINMENT FUNCTIONAL DESIGN REQUIREMENTS AND METRICS

Reliability

Reliability is critical to all four overarching goals for two reasons: its effect on a force's ability to accomplish missions and its effect on the resources, in terms of cost and footprint, required to restore and sustain weapon systems. The effect of reliability on the former can be measured in terms of MTBCF.[6] This metric should encompass inherent or true equipment failures, operational failures "induced" by operators or maintainers, and perceived but false failures. Design affects the frequency with which all three types of failures occur. When we think of design, we often think of the inherent reliability of the system, which is driven by the reliability of each component; how the components work together; and redundancy. Robust designs, though, are also less prone to operator- and maintainer-induced failures—this can be thought of as error proofing. In the design process, through an approach such as failure mode effects and criticality analysis (FMECA), the design team should identify all such potential failures and attempt to find ways to eliminate any that are critical and that have a reasonable probability of occurrence. Additionally, reliable built-in tests will minimize false failures. To an operator, when a built-in test indicates a failure and the system is thus taken off line, it is a true failure regardless of whether the system is later checked out as fully operational by maintenance. Consider a fire control failure indication: If you were a tanker, would you want to go into battle thinking your fire control computer was not working properly?[7]

While critical failures are of most interest to operators because they can affect mission accomplishment, logisticians are also concerned with noncritical failures because every type of failure produces resource demands: direct and indirect labor, spare parts, transportation, facilities, and training. Thus it is imperative to measure

---

[6]In this document, a critical failure is defined as a failure that makes an end item NMC.

[7]Programs might consider the use of three or even more submetrics for MTBCF, such as $MTBCF_i$ (inherent), $MTBCF_{in}$ (induced), and $MTBCF_f$ (false alarm) or false alarm rate (FAR), because they generally have different improvement paths.

mean time between maintenance actions (MTBM), which should be divided into MTBUM (unscheduled maintenance—what we think of when things break) and MTBSM (scheduled maintenance—what we think of when we bring our cars in for service or schedule a tank for overhaul), because they place different types of demands on the logistics system in terms of total resources and the ability to control when they occur. To the extent that scheduled maintenance can be smoothed, it reduces workload peaks, which can reduce the necessary maximum maintenance capacity. Scheduled maintenance also improves force design flexibility, because it can be executed by shared, nonunit resources and at the time and place of the Army's choosing. To fully understand and account for the effect of reliability on how resource requirements must be distributed across the logistics system, one needs to further divide MTBM metrics into measures by maintenance echelon.

Though not an element of reliability, maintenance actions resulting from combat damage also affect logistics resource requirements and can be measured as MTBM for combat damage (MTBMcd). Therefore, MTBMcd needs to be specified as an assumption in the equipment sustainment analysis to determine overall maintenance requirements. MTBMcd and MTBM should be analyzed separately in the equipment sustainment and survivability analyses to align metrics with development efforts.

Maintainability

Maintainability encompasses factors that affect the resources and time needed to complete repairs—including diagnosis and actual work—and capabilities that enable the logistics system to keep failures from affecting operations. Important questions are: How long does it take to do the repair work ("wrench-turning time"), on average? Are there any particularly difficult and time-consuming repairs? How much training is needed to complete repairs? What special tools and equipment are needed? The answers to these questions are affected, in part, by how components and subsystems, whichever represents the desired level of replacement, are packaged within the total system. How easy are they to get to (accessibility)? Are there any blind connections? How many and what types of fasteners are required? How heavy is each part? What special knowledge is necessary? Each of these questions must be answered from the perspective of both repairing equipment breakdowns and repairing battle damage.

Another key maintainability area is the quality of troubleshooting procedures, whether fully automated through sensors and built-in tests, completely manual using paper technical manuals, or something in between such as an expert system embedded in an electronic technical manual. How long does it take to troubleshoot problems? How successful are troubleshooting procedures the first time? Three metrics are necessary to assess the quality or effectiveness of diagnostics: fraction of faults detected (FFD) (of primary interest when evaluating automated diagnostics), fault isolation ratio (FIR)—does the procedure or automation isolate the fault to the specific item that must be replaced or repaired, and FAR—the percentage of failure indications when no failure has actually occurred. These three metrics can be combined into a composite metric— fraction of faults successfully diagnosed (FFSD) the first time. Misdiagnosis or a difficult diagnostic procedure can substantially lengthen the total downtime of a system. One or the other often drives the repair time variability, and they tend to lead to long repair actions.

Together, the workload and diagnostic factors affect maintenance man-hours per maintenance action, both unscheduled (MMH/UM) and scheduled (MMH/SM), again measured by echelon, and MTTR. Maintenance hours per event affects total resources (labor), and MTTR affects downtime duration or availability.[8] Because the maintenance demands are likely to be quite different, these metrics should be evaluated distinctly for repair actions driven by equipment failure and repair actions driven by combat damage.

Beyond affecting total force structure requirements, better maintainability can reduce footprint in the maneuver force. For example, if crews can repair a large percentage of faults, it would reduce the

---

[8]Maximum time to repair (MaxTTR) is also sometimes used as a requirement. It is an indication of any particularly difficult and time-consuming maintenance actions. Such maintenance actions should trigger attempted design improvements, whether to reduce the time to repair or to enable deferral until the end of a combat pulse. Used in this way, a program could use MaxTTR as a diagnostic metric to identify outlier repairs and continually drive down MTTR.

overall need for maintainers as well as those in the maneuver force. To encourage this, a metric such as the percentage of unscheduled maintenance actions that can be accomplished by the crew could be used. Parallel metrics would be the percentage of maintenance actions that are the responsibility of each echelon. The Combined Arms Support Command and the Army's Ordnance Center and School are developing a plan for a two-level maintenance system with on-system repair forward (usually remove and replace) and off-system repair rear—even with current systems that were not necessarily designed with these concepts in mind. Expressly designing new weapon systems to take advantage of new concepts will further enhance the effectiveness and value of such concepts.

Besides reducing total workload (total footprint and costs) and affecting workload distribution (footprint distribution), maintainability can play a role in reducing mission-critical failures, thereby improving pulse A_o, through prognostic technology that makes anticipatory maintenance feasible. The Army is making strong efforts to encourage the development and use of prognostics. The benefit of prognostics, though, is limited by the percentage of faults that can be predicted. Metrics parallel to the aforementioned diagnostic metrics can help quantify the potential benefit and help drive progress in this area. They are fraction of faults predicted (FFP) along with FIR and FAR. Similar to FFSD, a composite metric defined as fraction of faults successfully predicted could also be employed.

Fleet Life Cycle Management

Fleet life cycle planning assumptions and requirements should be explicitly recognized up front in program planning and resource allocation. To compute a meaningful life cycle cost requires a reasonable, supportable estimate of life cycle length. Any needs for recapitalization or major overhaul programs based on this life cycle length and the durability of the system's components should be explicitly forecast and recognized as a program requirement. Expected degradation in system failure rates over time should be accounted for—both in evaluating life cycle cost and determining reliability requirements—based upon component wear profiles and evaluations of similar systems/technologies in service. As part of this process, the program should consider durability and life cycle maintenance tradeoffs.

Estimates of reliability degradation as it affects mission-critical failures should be used in estimating pulse A_o. For example, if the Army expects a system to be in the fleet for 15 years before it is overhauled and an item suffers a 2 percent compound annual increase in the mission-critical failure rate, then the like-new reliability should be 35 percent higher than a calculated requirement that does not account for degradation ($1.02^{15} = 1.35$). To date, however, the Army does not have supportable estimates of how failure rates and support requirements increase over time.

A companion research task in the same project for which the research in this report has been executed is to develop estimates of the effects of aging on mission-critical failure rates and resource consumption. Initial findings from this research indicate that over the first fourteen years of the life of an Abrams tank, the mission-critical failure rate increases at a compound annual rate of about 5 percent, or about a doubling in expected failures for a given level of usage and environment (the data indicate that the aging effect most likely tails off soon after this range, as many of the components that contribute to the aging effect fail and are replaced—a process called renewal).

Much of the age effect comes from increases in the failure rates of simple components with dominant failure modes associated with fatigue. Examples include fittings, hydraulic hoses, and suspension components. This produces major changes in maintenance workload requirements, if not spare parts costs, and pulse A_o capabilities. If this result continues to hold as research progresses, it would be imperative to include life expectancy considerations in program planning. These considerations might include more frequent overhauls, akin to aircraft phase maintenance, and planned recapitalization programs.

Also of value, this study identifies two other categories of components that do not contribute substantially to the aging effect but are critical from a reliability standpoint. The first category consists of components with high failure rates regardless of age, making them pulse A_o drivers throughout a tank's life. The second category is medium- or high-failure-rate components with high unit prices, making them cost drivers.

Supply Support

In general, the spare parts supply chain is thought of as a broad system designed by the Army and DoD to support all weapon systems, so it is not generally thought of as an area that should have program-specific requirements. However, some systems are so significant or important to the Army's future that they may drive the entire support structure to begin a transition toward a new support concept. Similarly, a system may represent the first in a new generation of weapon systems that will necessitate a new support concept. From this vantage point, the support structure becomes integral to the total weapon system concept, and the Army may want to include any changes to the structure that are critical to making the concept successful.

Aside from this, program requirements always rest on some assumptions, often with regard to parts support. A key element of parts support that drives much of the differences in total repair time among weapon systems and units is the local authorized stockage list (ASL) fill rate—the percentage of requests that are immediately filled from a unit's supply support activity (SSA). Programs should set local fill rate performance requirements that support any assumptions made in the requirements determination process. The goals should not be to specify which and how many of each part, but rather to set an overall performance target for the local fill rate. This approach does not dictate the means, but rather the level of support that should be provided. Similarly, a level of wholesale spare parts performance could be specified. Again, this does not specify the means, such as whether parts have to be provided through organic or contractor support, only the performance to be expected in terms of having parts available for issue when needed.

Generally, the parts on deployable ASLs are for equipment failure-driven repairs. Separate requirements should be used for "battle damage parts kits" used to supplement ASLs for deployments. Such a requirement would have to be based upon assessments made during the development process as to what noncatastrophic damage may occur that would drive types of part replacements different from those normally caused by equipment failure.

One element of weapon system design that the Army can use to reduce the resource requirements necessary to provide a given level of parts support is part commonality. Using an extreme situation as an example, if ten different vehicles in a brigade used ten different chassis without common parts, there could be ten times as many unique parts as in a situation where all ten shared a common platform. Worse, it would be hard to support any of the ten very well, because the demand density at the part level for each vehicle type would be relatively low. Investments in spare parts can be a major cost contributor. Part commonality can also affect footprint, although spares are a relatively small portion of the total footprint. To drive progress on this front, the percentage of parts that are unique to the weapon system could be used as a metric. Of course, the Army must balance parts commonality against the unique requirements of each platform, depending upon tradeoffs between performance and commonality. An example of this type of thinking can be found in the auto industry, which often tries to create common platforms to reduce procurement and assembly costs. Some companies have gotten in trouble, though, when they took this concept too far. They made so many of their platforms common that they became indistinguishable, so people no longer bought the more expensive versions, viewing them as lacking sufficient performance differentiation to be worth the extra cost.

Army Interim and Objective Force planning efforts have also been exploring the use of spare "ready to fight" systems (RTFs) to replace broken or damaged weapon systems.[9] However, whether they would affect pulse A_o, pulse self-sufficiency, and maneuver force maintenance footprint depends primarily upon whether they would travel with the maneuver force or could be supplied during a combat pulse. And their value versus other resources (i.e., spare parts and maintainers) must be carefully analyzed for the relative benefits and

---

[9]A float is an additional or "spare" end item owned by an organization above and beyond the organizational structure requirement that can be used to replace a temporarily unavailable end item (or a permanently unavailable end item, which will require replacement of the float). Traditionally, brigades have small numbers of floats to replace end items that are expected to be down for an inordinate length of time. In contrast, ready to fight systems are viewed as another maintenance or readiness resource to be used when logistics resources become stretched during periods of high operating tempo.

costs. Additionally, RTFs could affect refit period length and refit effectiveness (and thus, indirectly, pulse A_o) assumptions.

A REVIEW OF ARMY ORDs

In a review of recent Army ORDs, we found that almost every requirement discussed in the previous section has been used for at least one weapon system program, but rarely do programs use a wide cross-section of them (see Appendix E for a list of ORDs reviewed). Instead, a couple are used in one program, another couple in another, and so forth, resulting in inconsistent use of these metrics. It appears that different groups in the Army have thought about the different parts of this list, but the Army as a whole has not constructed a comprehensive standard set of equipment sustainment metrics that could serve as a reference guide.

We now review the degree to which each of the metrics has been used to define program requirements. Table 3.3 provides a comparison of recommended requirements and metrics with those that have been used. Reliability and maintainability requirements have received the most attention among the categories we have discussed. Typically, some form of MTBCF appears in ORDs, although a variety of definitions and metrics are used.[10] The other common metrics used to define requirements are MTTR and the MR, which combines MMH per maintenance action and MTBM. Since it combines reliability and elements of maintainability, the MR represents a higher-level goal that translates to the number of maintainers required given the MMH per maintenance action and the OMS/MP. Thus it is a driver of footprint and cost. It is also fairly common for ORDs for replacement-type systems (those that are a direct replacement for another system in terms of function rather those that introduce fun-

---

[10]TRADOC has recently set mean time between system aborts (MTBSA) and mean time between essential function failure (MTBEFF) as standards. However, it has been suggested that other metrics continue to appear, because the starting point for an ORD is often the ORD for a similar, previously developed system. A system abort is a failure that prevents a system from being able to accomplish designated missions. Essential function failures are failures that degrade capability but do not prevent mission accomplishment or failures related to essential functions that do not impede operation in and of themselves. Combined with other EFFs, such failures could lead to system aborts. Examples include secondary sights and redundant circuit cards.

Table 3.3

A Comparison of Recommendations to Army ORDs

Requirement Category	Historical Use of Metrics for Equipment Sustainment Requirements	Potential Standard Metrics for Defining Sustainment Requirements
Availability	• Rare use of A_O • Rare use of "sortie" reliability (e.g., missile in-flight reliability)	• Pulse A_O (operational availability) — Use derived pulse A_i in some cases • Prob(successful sortie completion) • Specify pulse, refit, and sortie parameters[a]
Self-sufficiency	• Rare use of maintenance and spares self-sufficiency for a designated time period (e.g., 30 days) for a designated unit size	• Self-sufficiency pulse length
Equipment sustainment footprint	• Maintenance ratio and use of existing MOS, personnel, and equipment less/equal to current • Rare use of total deployment footprint	• Maintainers by echelon (cost and footprint driver); may be relative or maintenance ratio by echelon • Maintenance equipment lift requirements
Life cycle equipment sustainment cost	• SAR includes O&S costs • Use of O&S less/equal to current	• Total life cycle cost to "maintain" • Annual operation (cost per operating hour/mile) • Planned recapitalization • Spare parts provisioning • Investment in reliability (e.g., materiel)

Table 3.3—continued

Requirement Category	Historical Use of Metrics for Equipment Sustainment Requirements	Potential Standard Metrics for Defining Sustainment Requirements
Reliability	• Some form of MTBCF • Rare use of MTBM and MTBSM	• Standard form of MTBCF • MTBUM and MTBSM (by echelon)
Maintainability	• Recent use of FFP (very limited), FFD with FIR, FAR (very limited) • MTTR (sometimes by echelon) • MR (sometimes by echelon) • Rare use of MMH/SM • Miscellaneous features (e.g., org replaceable power pack) and rare use of percent UM-org level	• FFSP = Fn(FFP, FIR, FAR/NEOF Rate) • FFSD = Fn(FFD, FIR, FAR/NEOF Rate) • MTTR (by echelon) • MMH/UM (by echelon) • MMH/SM (by echelon) • Percent UM–crew, org, DS, GS
Fleet life cycle management	• Rare use (e.g., barrel life) • Plug in/plug out LRUs	• Specify replacement/recap/retirement schedule • Use estimate of reliability degradation in requirements analysis[a]
Supply support	• Rare use of fill rate requirements • Rare use of ALDT	• Local fill rate • Battle damage parts kit • Wholesale backorder rate • Percent of parts that are unique • Number and positioning of end item floats • Specify ALDT assumption[a]

[a]Critical assumptions that are necessary to determine the associated requirements.

damentally new capabilities or technologies) to specify that a system require the same number and type of personnel and equipment for support as those of the system it replaced.

A positive trend is that recent, major programs are making much greater use of diagnostic-oriented maintainability requirements, often using FFD and FIR metrics to define requirements. One ORD examined also used FFP and FAR. Many other ORDs recognize the need to use automated diagnostics that provide potential prognostic capability going forward, but until recently most just specified that the weapon system has to have built-in test/built-in test equipment (BIT/BITE) capability without quantifying the desired benefit.

In light of proposed Objective Force concepts that call for unit self-sufficiency during combat pulses, it is interesting to note that the requirements for one system currently in development include self-sufficiency without parts delivery or external maintenance support for a defined period. This was used in conjunction with a requirement for a specified level of local spare parts fill rate performance. Also of note is that one program specified a requirement for the percentage of maintenance actions that are within the capabilities of organizational-level maintenance, which is another type of requirement that may be of increasing interest as the Army strives to reduce maneuver force maintenance footprint.

While life cycle operating costs and other costs associated with life cycle support, such as for recapitalization, have traditionally not been stated as ORD requirements, they have been de facto requirements as a result of their inclusion in the Selected Acquisition Report (SAR). The SAR includes each major cost category.

Two major gaps consistently appear. The first is the lack of A_o usage or any other similar high-level metric directly related to warfighter mission needs. The absence of A_o, though, seems to be driven more by concerns with using it well, rather than whether it should be used at all. The second gap is the failure to explicitly treat changing maintenance demands over the course of a system's life. Such demands could be reflected in systematic degradation in pulse A_o and in increases in operating costs as reliability degrades as well as in preplanned recapitalizations to enable systems to meet operational and resource consumption goals over the full course of their service lives.

While pulse A_o is typically not used, the concept is often embedded in the requirements development process. To determine reliability and maintainability requirements, combat developments engineers must start from some higher-level goal. Often they target an average A_o over the time period and set of tasks specified in the OMS/MP. This is really an operational pulse, with the pulse length defined by the OMS/MP; thus the goal is pulse A_o. At other times the goal may be to keep a minimum number of systems, say four of six, available at all times over the series of tasks in the OMS/MP. This is akin to maintaining a minimum pulse A_o.

It seems that three factors then tend to combine to prevent carrying through the average or minimum pulse A_o target from reliability and maintainability requirements determination to inclusion as a program requirement. To derive reliability and maintainability requirements from an A_o target, ALDT (including spare parts) assumptions are necessary. The first factor has been a lack of good, supportable data to develop justifiable assumptions. The second is the inability to conduct a complete A_o test, which would have to include representative supply chain support. The third seems to be a hesitation to levy program requirements on internal DoD organizations.

To make the use of A_o viable, either A_o would have to be tested or it would have to be modeled using good assumptions. Additionally, it would probably require the use of some functional requirements that would be the responsibility of internal DoD organizations. While potentially difficult, these hurdles can be overcome. The next chapter includes a discussion of the pulse A_o evaluation problem.

Traditionally, requirements have been developed to serve as the basis of contractual specification for systems developers. They have been externally focused. However, requirements could also be used internally. Instead of being the basis for contractual specifications, they could form the basis of performance agreements accepted by organizational commanders. The resources to meet these performance agreements would be a necessary condition for the achievement of the performance targets. This would have the added benefit of helping to make support funding, such as for initial spare parts provisioning, and associated performance shortfalls more visible. In fact, the DoD as a whole is moving in directions that support this type of approach. The services are in the process of implementing performance-based logistics, which will consist of performance agreements between program managers and providers and their customers.[11] And the Defense Logistics Agency is planning to create performance agreements with its customers as it implements its Business Systems Modernization.

---

[11]E.C. Aldridge, Office of the Under Secretary of Defense for Acquisition, Technology, and Logistics, "Memorandum. Performance Based Logistics," February 13, 2002.

Chapter Four

LINKING DESIGN OBJECTIVES TO OVERALL GOALS

To make the use of overall goals feasible, we must understand the links between each design objective and each overall goal. In addition, it is critical to produce supportable estimates for each functional design parameter necessary to estimate the expected level of performance against each overall goal. This chapter describes how such linkage could occur and, using the example of pulse Ao, demonstrates the necessity of good estimates and assumptions.

LINKING DESIGN REQUIREMENTS TO HIGHER-LEVEL GOALS

High-level, overall goals are functions of equipment design and logistics system capabilities. Therefore, they are usually not directly testable (for example, the entire deployed logistics system cannot be set up in a test)—a reason sometimes given for not using Ao as a program requirement. However, this does not mean that they cannot be estimated reasonably well using a combination of simulation, testing, and empirical data analysis. Or a test could be conducted with processes outside of the scope of the physical test simulated through representative delays.

For each overall goal, there is a method for determining the value of the metric used to measure progress toward the goal, using the metrics that define the design objectives. These methods decompose the overall metrics to root-level design elements. As an example, Figure 4.1 provides a simple depiction of estimating pulse A_o, which is a function of the end item mission-critical failure rate and the total broke-to-fix time required to return items to mission-capable status.

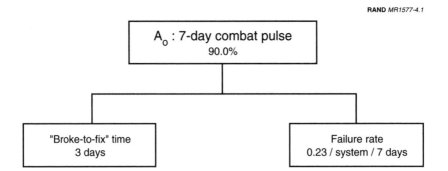

RAND *MR1577-4.1*

Figure 4.1—A Simple Model of Pulse A_o

Historically, though, methods for producing good, supportable estimates of broke-to-fix time have not been available. This has been the major issue preventing wider use of A_o.

We use pulse A_o as the example and focus on it in this chapter, because traditionally its use has been avoided owing to the aforementioned inability to measure it directly as well as the difficulty of developing good estimates through decomposition techniques. But if its subordinate metrics can be estimated well through supportable methods, then the use of A_o becomes viable, at least through evaluation techniques, if not actual testing.

DECOMPOSITION OF PULSE A_o

The metric "tree" presented in Figure 4.2 depicts an example decomposition of A_o into root process elements starting with total broke-to-fix time and the failure rate using a method developed through research sponsored by the Army's Deputy Chief of Staff, G-4.[1] Many of the root metrics are either not directly testable or are

---

[1]The Army's G-4 has been sponsoring a RAND Arroyo Center project titled "Diagnosing Equipment Serviceability." For a description of the equipment readiness diagnostic methodology developed through this research, see Eric L. Peltz, Marc L. Robbins, Patricia Boren, and Melvin Wolff, *Diagnosing the Army's Equipment Readiness: The Equipment Downtime Analyzer*, Santa Monica, CA: RAND, MR-1481-A, 2002.

RAND MR1577-4.2

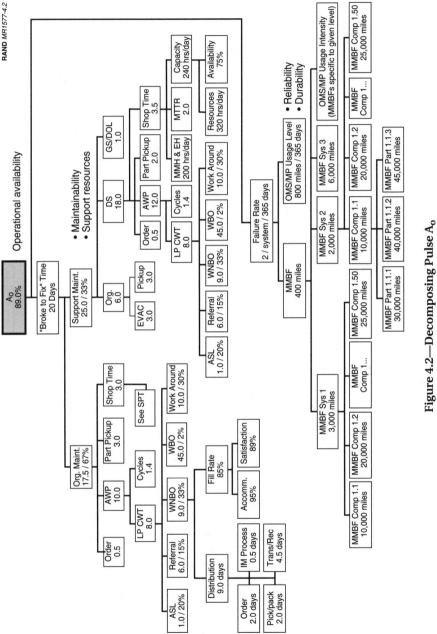

Figure 4.2—Decomposing Pulse A_o

beyond the scope of an individual weapon system (e.g., distribution time from a distribution center to a unit). So for this decomposition to be useful, assumptions have to be developed for such metrics, which might be done through empirical analyses and simulations. These assumptions and test and evaluation results (e.g., reliability and maintainability testing) associated with the metrics that define program functional requirements could serve as inputs to a simulation to determine pulse A_o. A first look at which techniques would be employed to develop estimates for each metric in this tree is provided in Appendix A.

As mentioned, one of the reasons for not using pulse A_o and not doing this decomposition in the past was the lack of supportable data for total broke-to-fix time and for many of its submetrics. However, over the last few years the Army has developed and fielded a variety of logistics information systems that provide data that could form the basis for developing better, empirically supported estimates of broke-to-fix time and its components. In particular, customer wait time (CWT) and stockage performance data should be very useful. And with the fielding of the Global Combat Support Systems–Army (GCSS-A), the data should further improve. Additionally, data from the Army Materiel Systems Analysis Activity's (AMSAA's) Field Exercise Data Collection (FEDC) and Sample Data Collection (SDC) system could be mined. FEDC and SDC data contain more detail than that collected through the Army's information systems, and the FEDC data offer the additional advantage of focusing on exercises at the National Training Center (NTC) and other locations.

Examining the various components of the overall goals has the added benefit of helping to better understand the program elements and equipment design features that have the most leverage on overall goals for a program. For instance, such analysis could show that significantly improving MTTR would have little influence on A_o, but dramatically improved FFP or ASL fill rates could have substantial influence. Then, emphasis could be placed on how to improve those logistics system elements or design features shown to have the ability to exert strong leverage. It is important, though, to ensure that each high-level goal is examined. For instance, in the example just described, MTTR could have great influence on maintenance footprint.

Generating Assumptions

The use of these new data sources, such as the CWT module in the Integrated Logistics Analysis Program (ILAP), should prompt a thorough scrubbing of traditional assumptions, which could lead to better recognition of the requirements necessary to achieve those assumptions or to actual changes in the values of assumptions employed in requirements determination. Figure 4.3 presents one such example. It is not unusual to see ALDT assumptions in the one- to four-day range used (and times as low as a few hours have been used as well) to determine reliability requirements. ALDT includes time spent waiting for parts.

In contrast, actual average Army CWT to deployed locations ranged from about 10 to 24 days in calendar year 2000, as depicted in the graph in Figure 4.3.2 CWT is now being measured by the Army from the time a customer enters a requisition in ULLS (organizational maintenance) or SAMS (support maintenance) until the SSA supporting the requisitioning maintenance activity issues the part and makes it available for pickup by maintenance personnel.3

However, the contrast between assumptions and actual CWT does not mean that traditional assumptions are necessarily wrong from a practical standpoint. This is because, as other recent RAND Arroyo Center research shows, the "effective CWT" from a maintenance perspective is often much shorter than the CWT when viewed from a supply system perspective. This difference results from workarounds such as controlled exchange (stripping a part from one down system to return another to mission-capable status).4 However, the Army should be sure it understands the root assumptions that would have to be met to achieve an ALDT assumption and then determine if these are reasonable. For example, an ALDT assumption may rest on very aggressive spare parts fill rate requirements and very high controlled exchange rates. If the root-level assumptions that are appro-

---

2CWT data, ILAP, February 2001 as posted on the Army's Velocity Management web site at *www.cascom.army.mil/VM.*

3Due to information system limitations, the last segment of CWT from SSA issue until pickup by maintenance cannot be measured. Nor is the time from when a crew realizes an item is NMC until the requisition is entered in ULLS measured.

4See Peltz et al., *Diagnosing the Army's Equipment Readiness,* op. cit.

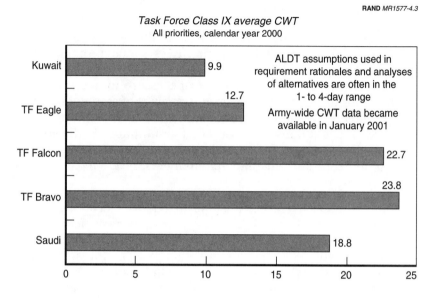

Figure 4.3—Actual CWT Performance to Deployed Locations

priate as requirements (e.g., fill rate) are specified as such and then
fully resourced, and if those that are not appropriate as requirements
(e.g., controlled exchange) are determined to be feasible, then the
overall ALDT assumption should be considered reasonable. Otherwise the assumption should reflect actual performance experienced
by the Army today (including the effect of workarounds, which can
be estimated fairly well). In the absence of a clear, resourced, and
validated plan to improve performance, the status quo performance
should be the conservative assumption.[5]

Data from the NTC might also be useful in assessing the reasonable-
ness of assumptions. For example, in fiscal year 1999, an average
ASL fill rate of 49 percent led to an average repair time of 2.9 days for
M1s and M2s during operational pulses (the 13 training days in the

_____

[5]TRADOC's Combat Developments Engineering Division has recently indicated that it
is beginning to use this approach. The division's management has stated that it will
start with actual CWT as the assumption, and changes to this assumption will have to
be justified. This is opposed to having to justify why actual CWT should be the
assumption.

maneuver "box"). An increase in the fill rate to 62 percent in fiscal year 2000 produced an average repair time of 2.2 days. These are probably lower bounds on the repair times for these levels of ASL performance, because the NTC is a one-day drive from its supporting wholesale distribution center and has a fairly robust infrastructure providing alternative means of procuring parts. Neither of these conditions is likely to be present in an actual deployment, at least in the early stages.

Demonstrating the Criticality of Assumptions

Figure 4.4 demonstrates why good assumptions are absolutely critical. Currently, even though pulse A_o is usually not used as a requirement, some form of availability is often used (something like pulse A_o is common) to determine reliability requirements. From the OMS/MP or Army policy or both (e.g., a goal of 90 percent operational readiness for ground systems), the requirements team determines the availability requirement. As discussed, A_o has two components: the failure rate and total broke-to-fix time. To determine the

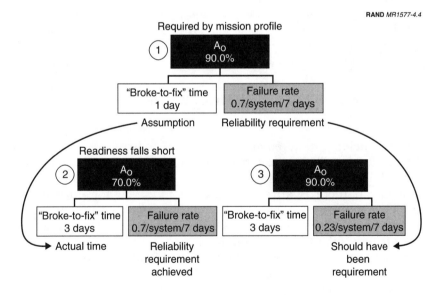

Figure 4.4—A Demonstration of the Criticality of Assumptions

required failure rate, which leads to the program reliability requirement, an assumption has to be made on how long it takes to return broken items to mission-capable status.

Suppose a program determines that a pulse A_o of 90 percent is necessary and the OMS/MP specifies a seven-day pulse length. If an average broke-to-fix time of one day is assumed (which is not unusual), then the failure rate requirement will be an average of 0.7 mission-critical failures per system over the seven-day pulse. From this and other information, one can determine a MTBCF requirement.

Now suppose that the program meets the reliability requirement of 0.7 failures per system per pulse, but instead of a broke-to-fix time of one day, it really turns out to be three days. The organization would experience a 70 percent A_o instead of 90 percent.

If a three-day broke-to-fix time assumption had been used, the reliability requirement would have had to be 67 percent better—0.23 failures per system per pulse—which would produce a MTBCF three times as high as the requirement based on the one-day assumption. Thus we see the criticality of good assumptions—in particular broke-to-fix times. Unrealistic assumptions can lead to requirements (such as for MTBCF), that even if met, do not produce the desired overall result (such as 90 percent pulse A_o). In other words, an unrealistically optimistic broke-to-fix time leads to a false and insufficient MTBCF requirement.

THE EFFECT OF A SELF-SUFFICIENCY REQUIREMENT ON PULSE A_o TESTING

A self-sufficiency requirement simplifies the pulse A_o test challenge. The biggest hurdle to conducting a full operational test of pulse A_o is an inability to replicate the full DoD parts distribution and supply system. If there is an operational requirement for pulse self-sufficiency, then this aspect of the problem goes away. During a pulse, the only logistics resources that would come into play are the maintainers, maintenance equipment, and spare parts that are integral to the maneuver force. While it would still require a heavily resourced test, it would be feasible to bring these elements together for an operational test.

Chapter Five

A FEW THOUGHTS ABOUT KPPs

This chapter briefly reviews DoD and Army KPP policy and then discusses how these policies might apply to equipment sustainment requirements. It also describes some alternatives to KPPs that might be used to drive the achievement of sustainability goals.

THE TECHNICAL ROLE OF KPPs

First, why are KPPs important (from the perspective of Acquisition Category 1 (ACAT 1) programs)?[1] The practical differences of KPPs as compared with other requirements are that they bring about congressional oversight and can trigger legally required program reviews. As a result, they represent truly hard constraints.

By strict policy, every threshold is technically a strict constraint—whether a KPP or not—but in practice there is some (and some would probably say substantial) room to modify non-KPP thresholds. Still, every requirement, whether a KPP or not, requires ORD approval authority to change, and as the result of a recent change, the ORD approval authority is the Chief of Staff of the Army (CSA).[2]

---

[1]ACAT I programs are Major Defense Acquisition Programs, which are either designated by the Under Secretary of Defense (Acquisition, Technology, and Logistics) (USD[AT&L]) as such or are estimated to require an eventual total expenditure for research, development, test, and evaluation of more than $365 million in fiscal year (FY) 2000 constant dollars or, for procurement, of more than $2.19 billion in FY 2000 constant dollars. They do not include highly sensitive classified programs.

[2]The CSA may delegate this authority on a program-specific basis, which, if done, would most likely be to either the Deputy Chief of Staff, G-3 (Operations and Plans), or the Commanding General of TRADOC.

Changing requirements

• All requirements require ORD approval authority (CSA) to change
  – Approval process includes FM FISO Team-led HQDA staffing and AROC review
  – Change authority can be delegated to the DCSOPS or CG, TRADOC
• For KPPs, JROC must also approve threshold changes (ACAT 1D)

Visibility

• KPP performance reported in DoD systems and to Congress
• Congress must be notified of intent to change KPP thresholds

Threshold deviations

• Any threshold deviation can be basis for delay, further testing, or conditional acceptance
• KPP shortfalls must be resolved or threshold changed (or OIPT change recommended for ACAT 1D) within 90 days or a formal program review must occur
• At FY end, if more than 10% of APB thresholds (including KPPs) are breached, there shall be a program review. The CAE (1C)/OIPT Leader (1D) with Vice Chairman of the JCS, shall determine if there is a continuing need for the program and recommend to the USD(AT&L) suitable actions, including program termination.

NOTE: This information pertains to ACAT 1 programs only, KPP status elevated through inclusion in APBs and SARs.

SOURCE: Interim Regulation, DoD 5000.2-R, January 4, 2001, Mandatory Procedures for Major Defense Acquisition Programs (MDAPs) and Major Automated Information System (MAIS) Acquisition Programs; DAMO-FM, The Army Requirements Process Information Briefing; CSA Memorandum, SUBJECT: Approval of Army Warfighting Requirements, March 19, 2001.

Figure 5.1—The Implications of KPPs

Prior to approval, requested changes must be broadly staffed across the Army Staff, the Army Secretariat, and Major Army Commands. A change then must be reviewed by the Army Requirements Oversight Council (AROC), which develops a recommendation for the CSA.[3] KPPs differ in this change process only formally in that if the program is an ACAT 1D, Joint Requirements Oversight Council approval is also necessary.[4]

---

[3]The AROC is chaired by the Vice Chief of Staff of the Army (VCSA) and includes the Deputy Chiefs of Staff for Operations and Plans (G-3), Programs (G-8), Personnel (G-1), Intelligence (G-2), and Logistics (G-4) as well as the Military Deputy to the ASA(ALT); the Director for Information Systems for Command, Control, Communications, and Computers; the Deputy Under Secretary of the Army for Operations Research; and the Deputy Chief of Staff for Developments, TRADOC.

[4]ACAT 1D programs are ACAT 1 programs for which the Milestone Decision Authority (MDA) is the USD(AT&L). For ACAT 1C programs the MDA is the DoD Component

Where KPPs differ from a more practical standpoint, however, is that performance against KPP thresholds is regularly reported to Congress, and Congress has to be notified of the intent to change a KPP because they must be included in the Acquisition Program Baseline (APB) and the SAR. Further, when the Program Manager has reason to believe that the current estimate of a KPP requirement would breach the threshold, the program has 90 days to get back on track or change the requirement (for a service-managed program) or to recommend a threshold change to the Overarching Integrated Product Team (OIPT) for Joint programs. Additionally, at a fiscal year's end, if more than 10 percent of an APB's thresholds are breached, a program review must occur.

Essentially, KPPs, because they can become politicized, are truly hard constraints, while a service retains some ability to manage tradeoffs internally among the other requirements—even beyond the thresholds. When doing so, the service still has the ability to delay a program until a shortfall is made up if a requirement's current estimate breaches a threshold, but it is also able to exercise judgment with regard to the benefit of doing so from the perspective of the total program and other performance estimates that are expected to be reached. A limited number of interviews suggested that programs have been delayed for non-KPP requirement shortfalls, including reliability. Alternatively, a program could be conditionally released based upon a plan to eliminate a shortfall.

ARMY AND DoD KPP SELECTION POLICY

This section reviews DoD and Army policy with regard to what requirements should be considered KPPs. The criteria are divided into two categories: intent and practicality. The intent criteria describe what they are supposed to represent from a theoretical standpoint. The practicality criteria ensure that they are usable and supportable.

At the most basic level, the set of KPPs for a program should describe the essence of the system—the most basic reason for why the system

---

Head or, if delegated, the DoD Component Acquisition Executive (CAE). All ACAT 1 programs are treated as ACAT 1D until formally designated ACAT 1C by the USD(AT&L).

is being developed. They should define what makes a system what it is and what should be essential for the system to accomplish its intended mission. KPPs should directly reflect specified operational or overall goals, which means they are often high-level composite metrics that permit tradeoffs among subordinate design objectives. Because KPPs firmly constrain the tradespace, programs are advised to minimize the number of KPPs as much as possible while ensuring that all completely essential requirements to make a weapon system valuable are KPPs.

Beyond meeting these intent criteria, KPPs need to be practical. The first issue that must be considered is whether there is a definable threshold that can be clearly justified as a hard constraint. Second, there must be an effective means of reliably assessing whether the threshold is being met. Third, a KPP must be technically and financially feasible. This last requirement, combined with the importance of most major programs to the proponent service, may induce conservative behavior when setting KPP thresholds.

Examples of KPPs

To help illuminate what the KPP policy criteria signify, this report provides two examples. The root mission need of the recently selected Interim Armored Vehicle (IAV) is to provide a family of vehicles (FOV) that are air transportable anywhere in the world and support infantry operations. From this definition, four KPPs result. The first is Command, Control, Communications, Computers, Intelligence, Surveillance, and Reconnaissance (C4ISR) interoperability, which is a KPP currently mandated by DoD policy. The second is to be transportable in a C-130, which is triggered by the "anywhere in the world" requirement. The third, specific to the Infantry Carrier Vehicle (ICV) and Engineer Support Vehicle (ESV) configurations, is to be able to carry an infantry squad. The fourth, for the Medium Gun System (MGS) variant, is to be able to destroy a standard infantry bunker (defined in the ORD) and produce an opening through which infantry can pass. Each of these relates directly to the basic justification for procuring the IAV. Note that each KPP is measured using a binary metric—can or cannot the IAV do a particular task?

In contrast, continuous variables are often viewed as having the practical issue of defining a precise, logical threshold. We use as the second example a program that effectively used KPPs measured with continuous variables, but ones in which the threshold had a clear physical basis. The M88A2 HERCULES recovery vehicle was developed to recover and evacuate a 70-ton combat-loaded M1A2 Abrams Main Battle Tank. Thus it had to have towing, braking, lifting, and winching capacities based on a 70-ton tank. In effect, each KPP translates a requirement to accomplish a specific task into a more generic functional capability requirement that can be evaluated using a traditional measurement. Using a continuous measurement instead of a binary one makes it easier to understand and communicate how an achieved capability compares with a required capability. For example, a tester can tell design engineers whether a winching capability shortfall is one ton short of the requirement or two—not just that it cannot winch the tank.

However, these "clean" examples of cut-and-dried thresholds for KPPs are based upon simplistic descriptions. In practice, there is almost always some gray area when defining thresholds. For example, for the IAV, one has to determine what a standard infantry bunker is, the size of a infantry squad (number of people and soldier "size" limits, if any) and what it carries, and whether the vehicle has to fit in a C-130 without any modification or preparation. In the HERCULES case, specifications for performance against these KPPs also had to include parameters such as the maximum grade for towing and how situational factors (e.g., whether a tank to be recovered is stuck in mud or on level, dry ground) should apply.

THE MERIT AND ISSUES OF RECOMMENDED REQUIREMENTS AS KPPs

We now view equipment sustainment metrics through the lens of the policy criteria just discussed. In line with the criterion to employ the highest-level composite metrics possible, we limit the review to the overall goals, which are composites of reliability, maintainability, fleet life cycle management, and supply support requirements.

From an intent standpoint, pulse A_0 has potential merit as a KPP, because it is a direct operational goal. If the mission need dictates that some level of availability is necessary or the Army can define at what point a force becomes combat ineffective and can no longer accomplish its mission, then pulse A_0 would be a viable KPP. In some cases, this need is relatively transparent, in particular for cases in which availability must be very high. Such cases might include essential "on call" systems (e.g., a missile defense system) or a critical low-density system that enables the rest of the force (e.g., a UAV without end item redundancy that provides the eyes for the shooting systems in the FCS). For other systems, there is certainly always a point in terms of availability at which a combat force would be combat ineffective; determining this level, though, often requires a rigorous operational analysis, based on the organizational architecture and what makes this architecture effective. What are the critical capabilities that make an organization combat effective? At what echelon/unit size does it make sense to measure availability from a combat effectiveness standpoint? Once this is understood, the individual system availability necessary to keep this level of organization combat effective can be determined. The next section illustrates these issues.

Once these questions are answered, the issue with pulse A_o remains whether a program could clearly define, up front, a logical, justifiable threshold beyond which a system would not be worth buying. Say a program determines that going below 70 percent pulse A_o would make a combat force ineffective. If the program came in at an estimate of 69 percent, would the Army want to face the prospect of having the program reviewed? What if it were 68 percent? Assuming the rest of the program's elements were doing well, it is likely the Army would want to continue the program but search for a means to make up the shortfall. A KPP designation would then force the development of a solution path. This is where the benefit of using a composite performance requirement, such as availability, versus a one-dimensional design characteristic, such as reliability, becomes apparent. In essence, not meeting the threshold indicates that the selected concept does not quite provide the expected and needed performance. With a composite requirement, though, multiple options remain for closing this gap—either finding a way to resolve shortfalls in individual design characteristics or modifying the concept.

On the other hand, one might argue that there is not a clear cutoff with regard to a requirement such as availability beyond which a program is not worth considering. However, it is hard to come up with any requirement without any gray area. Generally, the "boundary conditions" represent gray areas in even seemingly straightforward situations that allow for some "tweaking." For example, the requirement for a combat vehicle to be deployable in a given aircraft presents some gray areas in size and weight based upon aircraft range, flying conditions, what is on the vehicle, etc. However, these choices are generally more at the margins and insufficient to, say, justify putting a M1A1 on a C-130. Likewise, one can argue about whether 70 percent or 69 percent pulse A_o is right, but the choice between 50 percent and 70 percent should be clear. At some point, leaders must judge whether a requirement is being stretched or broken.

If the plan to support an end item evolves into a situation in which no repair is possible during a combat pulse, then pulse A_o devolves to pulse reliability. This would become the key measure of merit, as it alone would determine pulse A_o.

As the Army begins to think more broadly about procuring weapon systems as part of a larger integrated force or systems of systems, it is recognizing that combat power and force effectiveness go even further beyond the pure firepower and movement capabilities of its combat platforms than previously thought. The total mobility of the force—at tactical, operational, and strategic levels—is a critical factor in bringing combat power to bear at the right place at the right time. An increasingly recognized way to maximize the combat power that can be brought to bear is to minimize the footprint of all elements of a force that do not directly add combat power in terms of firepower and maneuver—such as the maintenance footprint—so that the amount of combat power deployable by a given amount of deployment throughput capacity is maximized. This also increases the operational mobility of a maneuver force. Thus, as footprint reduction has become an important high-level goal of the Army's Transformation, a footprint requirement meets the intent criteria of KPP policy. To develop a threshold, the Army could assess the throughput available for deployment and then, in conjunction with the deployment time goal and the footprint allocation for other force elements, determine the limit of the CSS footprint (including the maintenance footprint). Regardless of the footprint metric chosen, the determined threshold, in conjunction with a pulse A_o requirement (whether a KPP or not), would guide the determination of design objectives for reliability, maintainability, fleet life cycle management, and supply support capabilities.

Combat pulse self-sufficiency has become embedded in Objective Force operational thinking because, by enabling nonlinear operations with their attendant noncontiguous lines of communication, in conjunction with envisioned battlefield lift assets such as the joint transport rotorcraft and very high speed and agile combat platforms, it enables unprecedented tactical and operational freedom of action. Thus self-sufficiency during combat pulses would meet the intent criteria if Objective Force nonlinear concepts become doctrine. From a maintenance perspective, the threshold is simply "no delivery of parts or maintenance support from units outside the maneuver force during pulses." This becomes a support concept that again, in conjunction with both availability and footprint requirements, drives the needed levels of subordinate requirements such as reliability.

Since life cycle cost elements are included in the SAR, which is sent to Congress, life cycle cost automatically plays a role similar to a KPP in every program whether or not it is actually included as a requirement in an ORD. However, in a number of briefings, consistent, adamant feedback has been received that life cycle costs are treated and estimated very poorly during programs. On the surface, this appears to be a problem of execution and not policy. The extent to which recent programs have considered the spectrum of life cycle operating and support costs deserves further research by the Army. Briefing feedback suggests that some costs are often not considered: other equipment (e.g., new recovery vehicles), recapitalization over the expected life cycle of the fleet, replacement requirements over the expected life cycle of the fleet, annual military maintenance labor hours, and technical data packages.

What Is Combat Effective?

Figure 5.2 illustrates some of the issues with regard to defining combat effectiveness. We pose two questions: Are there clear rules for defining combat effectiveness at different echelons? At what echelon of organization is it most appropriate or meaningful to think about combat effectiveness? We present these questions from a legacy

RAND MR1577-5.2

Combat effectiveness status at various echelons by day
(80% overall A_O with downtime randomly distributed)

Day	1	2	3	4	5	6	7	8	9	10	Avg "Readiness"
44 tanks	95%	84%	91%	75%	77%	80%	66%	82%	73%	75%	80%
1/A	100%	75%	100%	75%	75%	100%	75%	75%	50%	50%	80%
2/A	100%	75%	50%	75%	75%	100%	75%	75%	25%	75%	80%
3/A	100%	100%	100%	75%	77%	50%	25%	50%	100%	75%	70%
HQ/A	50%	100%	50%	50%	100%	100%	50%	100%	50%	0%	
1/B	100%	75%	100%	75%	75%	100%	75%	75%	100%	75%	100%
2/B	100%	100%	100%	100%	25%	50%	75%	100%	75%	100%	80%
3/B	100%	75%	75%	75%	100%	100%	50%	100%	75%	100%	90%
HQ/B	100%	100%	100%	50%	100%	100%	50%	100%	50%	50%	
1/C	100%	75%	100%	50%	100%	50%	100%	100%	75%	100%	80%
2/C	75%	75%	100%	100%	75%	75%	100%	100%	100%	50%	90%
3/C	100%	75%	100%	75%	50%	75%	75%	75%	100%	100%	90%
HQ/C	100%	100%	100%	100%	100%	100%	0%	50%	50%	100%	
HQ	100%	100%	100%	50%	100%	50%	50%	50%	50%	50%	
Companies											
A Co	3	3	2	3	3	2	2	2	1	2	90%
B Co	3	3	3	3	2	2	2	3	3	3	100%
C Co	3	3	3	2	2	2	3	3	3	2	100%
BN	3	3	3	3	3	3	3	3	2	3	100%

Notional "combat effectiveness" rules

Medium – Combat effective (platoon at 100% FMC, 3 PLT/CO, 3 CO/BN)
Light – Combat effective – degraded (platoon at 75% FMC, 2 PLT/CO, 2 CO/BN)
Dark – Combat ineffective (platoon at 50% or less FMC, <2 PLT/CO, <2 CO/BN)

Figure 5.2—An Illustration of Alternative Methods for Defining Combat Effectiveness in Terms of Equipment Availability

force perspective, while noting that an FCS-based force poses additional considerations, in particular the relationships among different system types.

We examine the daily operational availability of an armor battalion's tanks over 10 days and compare various levels of metrics. Traditionally, availability-based measures (which include standard monthly readiness reporting) are simply an average of the availability of each individual system in the organization being assessed, whether a battalion, division, or some other unit size. This type of measure is depicted in the first row of the chart. In this case, such a measure produces an 80 percent 10-day pulse A_o across the 44 tanks of the battalion. However, the distribution of failures was such that on one day the A_o was just 66 percent (see row 1), which falls below the 70 percent threshold that is a commonly used assumption with regard to a force being combat effective or not.[5] So by this measure, the battalion would have been deemed combat effective on 9 of 10 days.

We now apply the 70 percent threshold of combat effectiveness from a maneuver element basis (e.g., the percentage of combat effective platoons or companies) rather than through an equipment-oriented metric (percentage of tanks in the battalion operational). First, we look at each platoon. Platoons are indicated by the platoon number and then the company, e.g., 1/A is 1st Platoon of Company A, with the three platoons of each company followed by the company headquarters sections. In this notional example, a platoon has to have three operational tanks to be considered a viable maneuver element that can accomplish typical platoon mission-essential tasks and thus be combat effective. Medium shading and 100 percent A_o indicate days on which platoons are at 100 percent effectiveness. Light shading and 75 percent A_o indicate days on which they could be degraded, depending upon the tasks to be accomplished (e.g., some tasks may be more dependent on the total amount of direct fire that can be brought to bear than others). And dark shading (25 percent or 50 percent A_o) indicates days on which platoons are combat ineffective by this standard. Every platoon except one has at least one day in which it is combat ineffective.

---

[5]During NTC rotations, 70 percent availability for a battalion's weapon system fleet is considered the standard. Units can be forced to cease training if their A_o falls below this level and stand down for maintenance to bring A_o back up to an acceptable level.

Next we examine the company level. In assessing company-level combat effectiveness, we base the assessment on the number of viable platoon-size maneuver elements. The assumption made here is that a company can perform mission-essential tasks if it has two or more effective platoons, and that when it has only two it might suffer some level of degradation. In this example, there is only one day on which one company is combat ineffective by this standard—A Company on day 9. Note, though, that if the 1st and 2nd Platoons in A Company had cross-leveled their tanks on day 9, they could have formed one platoon with three operational tanks, which would have resulted in A Company being considered mission effective. While the company would certainly be degraded for many missions with only 8 of its 14 tanks operational, it is conceivable that it could still be assigned some company-level tasks.

Now turn to the battalion level. Instead of looking at the A_o based on a simple count of how many of the 44 tanks are operational, we assess battalion-level effectiveness as a function of the number of effective company-sized maneuver elements it has (bottom row of Figure 5.2). The assumption made is that if there are two or more effective companies, then the battalion can still be mission effective (again, with only two companies, some level of degradation occurs, and some degradation exists when there are three companies at less than full strength). By this standard, even without the cross-leveling in Company A, the battalion would be deemed mission effective on each of the 10 days.

How "ready" to fight was this battalion? What is the "right" number? By the most traditional measure and in line with how readiness is measured, availability was 80 percent. Using a battalion fleet average, but by day instead, produces 90 percent. Using platoon-ready days, the number is 84 percent. Using company-ready days, it is 97 percent (or 100 percent with cross-leveling among platoons). Using battalion-ready days developed through the mission-effectiveness rules results in a 100 percent measurement.

While this figure begins to illustrate the complexity of the issues with regard to defining combat effectiveness, it also suggests the beginnings of a potential framework for doing so. One might start with the mission-essential task list for each unit size and assess the minimum number of end items or submaneuver elements it must have to even think about trying to execute all of the tasks or a minimum subset of assigned tasks. At each level, one could decide whether it is important to know how many total systems are available or how many subelements are viable maneuver elements. Or a combination of both could be used. If a set of supportable rules could then be defined for assessing combat effectiveness, the Army would have the means to define clear, hard thresholds for pulse A_o requirements. Regardless of the level this would be defined at, combat development engineers could then calculate the required availability at the system level necessary to reach this unit goal. A standard such as having a 95 percent (or 99 percent) probability that a battalion would be combat effective (100 percent of its companies available to execute company-level tasks) over all seven days of a combat pulse could be used. From this standard, a system pulse A_o requirement could be derived.

The key is whether clear thresholds of capability can be identified. Think of it like this: A four-tank platoon can have 0, 25, 50, 75, or 100 percent A_o at any given time. While it does have some value or combat power at 25 or 50 percent A_o, the question becomes whether the value is so low from a platoon standpoint that it becomes reasonable to represent it as zero value. Are there some platoon tasks that the platoon cannot even attempt to execute? Or at what point would the leaders or the personnel in the crews of still-operational tanks decide that it no longer makes sense to try to execute an assigned mission because the risk is too high? While more typically thought of from a combat damage sense, the notion of breakpoints may have some applicability to total availability as well—that is, availability associated with both combat and maintenance losses. If a company were attacking a position, at what point in terms of losses, both combat and maintenance, would it decide to break off the attack and regroup? Identifying such step functions in mission capability would strengthen the justification for availability thresholds.

SOME FINAL THOUGHTS ON KPPs

In the Army there has been a debate about whether reliability should be a KPP for the FCS. No one argues whether reliability is important, and it is not difficult to show, as in Chapter Two, that reliability and other sustainment issues are very important. What is difficult to show is how the importance of reliability or even a higher-level metric such as availability compares in importance to other performance parameters such as lethality, survivability, and mobility. In fact, we have not seen any studies that make this comparison. It would be valuable to study the relative influence on combat outcomes of sustainment capability and other elements of performance in order to develop insights or general conclusions with regard to the relative value of sustainment performance vice other performance goals through high-resolution combat simulations.

When thinking about KPPs, it is important to remember that there are two, albeit potentially dependent, decisions involved. One is whether to make a requirement a KPP. The other is to determine the threshold value. Making something a KPP does not necessarily make the threshold high; it just makes it a firmer constraint. A desire for an aggressive advance in performance probably should not be reflected as a KPP, unless a system is only valuable if such an aggressive advance can be achieved. Then the Army should recognize and communicate to others that it is pursuing a high-risk, high-payoff system and be prepared to accept the fact that the system will not be pursued if the desired advance is not achieved.

Since a KPP should only be based upon feasible thresholds, if an advance in performance is desired in a potential KPP parameter, significant emphasis should be placed on general science and technology and early concept development efforts oriented on improving the feasible performance and thus the feasible threshold value. The greatest potential for increasing sustainment performance may lie in what the Army can do, both in general or early in programs, to influence the feasible bounds on capabilities before an ORD must be approved.

OTHER MEANS FOR INCREASING THE IMPORTANCE OF EQUIPMENT SUSTAINMENT REQUIREMENTS

Part of the argument for making an equipment sustainment requirement a KPP is the belief that increasing the importance of a requirement is an effective way of driving improvement. There is probably significant merit to this belief. However, as we have just discussed, making something a KPP does not necessarily imply aggressive performance improvement; rather, it makes achieving a goal essential. So the question becomes whether this is the best method for raising the importance of a requirement in all instances or whether there might be alternative, and in some cases even better, approaches. For example, achieving a level of equipment sustainment capability above the level deemed necessary to make an individual weapon system worth procuring could produce substantial benefit from a total Army standpoint. In this case, a method besides making an equipment sustainment requirement a KPP becomes necessary to spur progress toward this valuable, higher level.

The following discussion suggests a few alternative, potential policies and strategies that employ leadership "signals" to drive desired Army management and contractor behavior, provide means for increasing process discipline, or create financial leverage. As is sometimes done today, equipment sustainment requirements can be designated as milestone exit criteria in the acquisition process, raising the visibility of performance against these requirements as well as the visibility of the decisionmaking process when shortfalls occur. This provides an opportunity for senior leaders to demonstrate their commitment to improving equipment sustainment performance, yet it still retains some flexibility for further exploration of the tradespace in the decisionmaking process.

Similarly, the prominence of these requirements has been increased through mandatory inclusion in AROC briefings, and the same could be done at milestone decision review briefings and other key meetings. Briefing requirements could include not only performance against overall goals but also how the system will affect progress toward achieving the Army's CSS Transformation.

A third option for increasing the emphasis on equipment sustainment requirements would be to increase their importance in the test and evaluation process. Formally increasing their use as critical operational issues would directly influence a program. Increasing test and evaluation resources would have an indirect influence by demonstrating the value that the Army places on achieving equipment sustainment requirements. Increased test and evaluation resources could also play a direct reliability and maintainability improvement role by better enabling the identification of specific design enhancement opportunities and issues through a maturational development process.[6]

Increasing the visibility and importance of equipment sustainment requirements in the Army works by attempting to influence those in the Army responsible for managing programs and contractors. Alternatively, the Army could employ direct means of influencing contractors. For example, the Army could tie financial incentives, such as award fees, to achieving equipment sustainment performance that exceeds threshold requirements. Structured properly, such financial incentives could have a net positive financial effect on the Army resulting from reduced life cycle sustainment resource requirements. Another method would be to increase the emphasis on evaluations of contractor past performance and product development management practices when selecting contractors.

One might note that the potential policies and strategies outlined here are of two types: some incentivize maximum possible performance, and others impose additional process discipline, albeit short of that imposed by a KPP (which preserves additional flexibility for the Army's senior leadership to exercise judgment when making decisions).

---

[6]See John Dumond et al., *Maturing Weapon Systems for Improved Availability at Lower Costs*, Santa Monica, CA: RAND, MR-338-A, 1994.

Chapter Six

APPLYING THESE CONCEPTS TO FCS CONCEPT DEVELOPMENT

This chapter further illuminates some of the concepts discussed, using FCS conceptual development as an example. It begins with data collected on legacy systems as a way of illustrating the need for tradeoffs and a balanced approach to sustainability development. Then the discussion moves to the FCS and the possibility that the system could require higher platform availability or greater redundancy than legacy weapon systems because of its dependence on networks.

"ULTRA" RELIABILITY WAS INITIALLY PROPOSED AS A SOLUTION PATH

We first return to the operational assumptions of the Objective Force. These assumptions *initially* led to extreme assumptions with regard to implications for logistics concepts. Specifically, this included no maintenance and supply units in the maneuver force. This led to an assumption made by some that there would be no repair in a maneuver force during combat pulses, which in turn led to the assumption that it would be necessary to rely solely on reliability to achieve the desired level of availability during a combat pulse.[1] Since with this series of assumptions reliability becomes the sole means of achieving pulse availability, this implies that pulse reliability and thus inherent design reliability must be extremely high. Even

---

[1]While having no maintainers in the maneuver force was initially discussed, it is no longer treated as viable, and draft Objective Force maneuver unit designs have maintainers, albeit very few.

though these assumptions are no longer treated as a possibility, we explore the implications to illustrate the need for using the broad tradespace discussed in this report, which is the direction in which the FCS program has moved.[2]

An Example of Pulse Reliability

Figure 6.1 presents pulse reliability data gathered at NTC from rotations 98-10 to 02-10, with each column depicting the performance of one Armor battalion over the course of one rotation. The columns indicate the battalions' seven-day tank pulse reliability (the percentage of tanks that made it through the first seven days without failing). Five battalions brought relatively new M1A2s to NTC, and four battalions brought their M1A1s. All others employed NTC prepositioned M1A1s. The FCS ORD currently calls for three-day high-intensity pulses and seven-day low-intensity pulses. As discussed earlier, projected Objective Force operating tempo is much higher than even NTC tempo. Therefore, the seven-day NTC pulse reliability is used for comparison.

The average seven-day pulse reliability for the two M1A2 rotations was 58 percent. Based upon this percentage, it would take a fivefold increase in the MTBCF for M1A2s to achieve 90 percent pulse reliability, and current FCS planning translates to a 95 percent pulse reliability requirement if no repair occurs during pulses. The M1A1s averaged about 37 percent seven-day pulse reliability, which would require a ninefold increase in MTBCF to reach 90 percent pulse reliability, and the one-day M1A1 pulse reliability was just 87 percent. Even for relatively new M1A2s, there is a significant gap between reliability and the requirements that must be met to make a system without any repair in the maneuver force viable. And if combat damage was accounted for, the gap would be even larger. The first key question these numbers raise is whether the gap can be closed in one generation of weapon system design and fielding.

---

[2]Even without maintainers, this assumption may have been questionable, since crews, especially with good design for maintainability, can do some, or even extensive, maintenance.

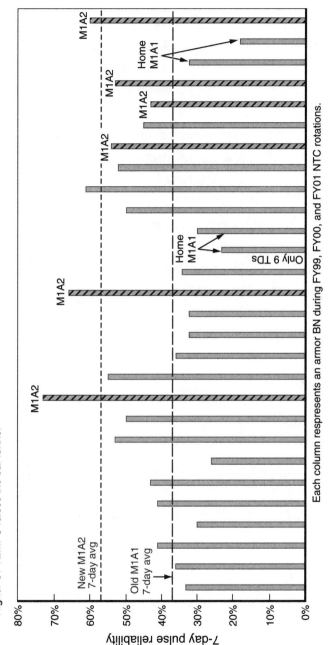

- Future systems, even if "ultra-reliable" will integrate with legacy systems
- What is a feasible range of reliability improvement to make in one generation of weapon systems?
- How does an "ultra-reliability" requirement affect the useful life? O&S costs?
- Higher OPTEMPO raises the bar further

Each column respresents an armor BN during FY99, FY00, and FY01 NTC rotations.

Figure 6.1—M1 Abrams Reliability at the NTC

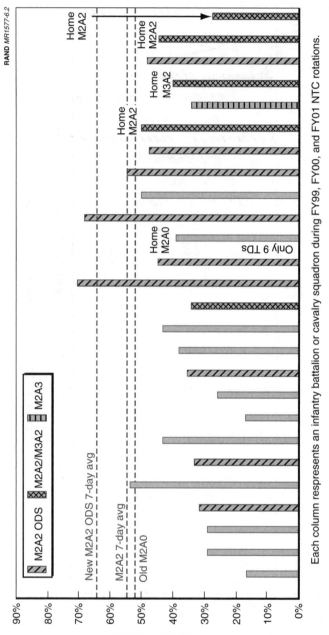

Each column respresents an infantry battalion or cavalry squadron during FY99, FY00, and FY01 NTC rotations.

Figure 6.2—M2 Bradley Pulse Reliability at the NTC

To the extent that the much worse M1A1 performance is attributable to age, it raises serious questions about the Army's ability to depend just on system reliability to maintain available equipment during combat pulses. Not only must new systems reach the goals, but so too must old ones, which would either set the "out of the box" reliability goal even higher or demand more frequent overhaul or recapitalization programs. So the second key question becomes whether—even if a new system is sufficiently reliable to eliminate the need for maintenance during combat pulses—this level of reliability can be sustained over a system's life. Additionally, to avoid repair totally, every major end item in a force would have to meet a very high reliability standard.

Similar analysis for the M2 Bradley at NTC (Figure 6.2) indicates a need for a fourfold increase in reliability over relatively new M2A2ODS to achieve 90 percent pulse reliability over seven days and a sixfold increase over older M2A2s and M2A0s.

FCS Performance Improvements

Figure 6.3 (based on FCS program presentations from FCS Industry Day and the FY 2000 Army Science Board Summer Study) presents those areas in which the Army is aiming for aggressive step-change performance improvements and how the Army thinks such improvements might be achieved. For most key areas for which the Army has targeted dramatic improvement, at least one technological step change–producing solution—sort of a silver bullet–type solution—has been identified that, if successfully brought to production, will do much to help the Army reach the target. Some are still in early development and feasibility is not certain, but at least the possibility exists.

Contrast these solutions with those identified for reliability improvement. There are many good ideas and proven practices for improving reliability, but they operate through a process-driven approach, which is often more evolutionary than revolutionary in nature. Over time, evolutionary improvements can produce revolutionary change, but it often takes continuous improvement through many iterations. Product development organizations must learn how to develop more reliable equipment. This is not to say there are no product technology solutions on the horizon—there are.

RAND *MR1577-6.3*

Fuel: weight from 70 tons to 20 tons, hybrid diesel-electric, fuel cells

Water: battlefield generation from diesel exhaust

Ammunition: precision munitions, brilliant munitions

Lethality: advanced KE missiles, HIMARS, E-FOGM and CMFSV, electromagnetic gun, advanced conventional guns and warheads, brilliant munitions

Survivability: lightweight passive armor, smart armor, active protection

Mobility: robotics, JTR

Reliability:

• Process driven approach (design and program management)

  – Enhanced use of product design methods (PoF, FMECA, etc.)

  – Fewer parts

  – More effective use of integrated teams earlier in design process

  – Increased management emphasis

  – Increased use of simulation

  – Improved contracting

  – Better, earlier testing

  – Often characterized by continuous incremental change

• Distributed solutions (subsystems and thousands of components)

  – Digital LRUs, multiplexing, advanced materials, and sensors offer potential

Figure 6.3—A Comparison of Solutions for FCS Performance Increases Among Functional Dimensions

However, dramatic reliability improvement requires improving a host of subsystems and thousands of dissimilar components (e.g., hydraulics, electronics, mechanical parts, sensors, etc.). A solution must be identified for each, and the technology solutions, unlike the process approach, may result in higher cost (expensive electronics, sensors, advanced materials, or redundancy) or higher weight (e.g., beefier suspension components) that in some cases produce deployability and fuel-efficiency tradeoffs.

THE BROADER TRADESPACE

Without the possibility of a broader tradespace to achieve availability goals (i.e., a reliability-centric solution path), the reliability "gap" between current systems and what is needed (if no repair were to occur during combat pulses) begins to make initial Objective Force sus-

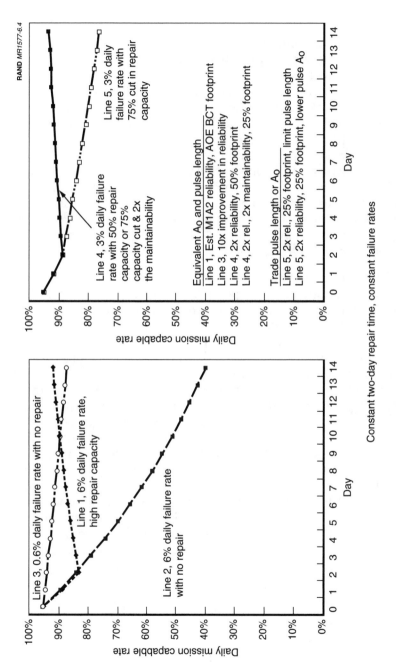

Figure 6.4—Illustrating the Equipment Sustainment Tradespace

tainment concepts appear high risk. Let us relax the no-repair assumption for a moment and see what we can learn. First look at line 1 on the left graph of Figure 6.4, which depicts daily A_o over a two-week combat pulse for a unit. The unit suffers a failure rate of about 6 percent of its available equipment each day (similar to the M1A2 failure rate at NTC) after starting at 95 percent A_o, but it has sufficient repair capacity to quickly return these items to mission capable status. This example assumes a constant two-day repair time. The result of these assumptions is line 1, which stays relatively close to 90 percent availability each day (not unlike the experience of the M1A2 battalions at NTC during FY 2000). If the unit did not repair any items during the pulse, the result would be line 2. To get something like line 1, but without repair, would require an order-of-magnitude increase in reliability—from 6 percent to 0.6 percent of the fleet failing per day, as indicated by line 3.

Now we look at the right graph, starting with line 4. In this case, the failure rate improves by 50 percent, equivalent to a twofold improvement in MTBCF, and repair capacity drops by half. This balanced approach, with still substantial footprint reduction, achieves the same A_o result as an order-of-magnitude improvement in reliability, and a balanced approach is probably much more feasible while still producing substantial gain. Note that this improvement occurs with only a cut in repair capacity. Any improvement in design for maintainability could further cut the need for repair capacity and footprint. For example, line 4 could also represent a scenario in which there is a twofold improvement in MTBCF, a twofold improvement in maintainability, and a 75 percent reduction in repair capacity. Another option in the tradespace would be to accept some availability degradation as depicted by line 5. This line shows the daily A_o with the same twofold improvement in reliability and three-fourths cut in repair capacity (again without any improvement in maintainability). The final option illustrated, also through line 5, would be to cut back on the pulse length, to three or four days in this example, which would enable end-of-pulse availability to stay close to 90 percent.

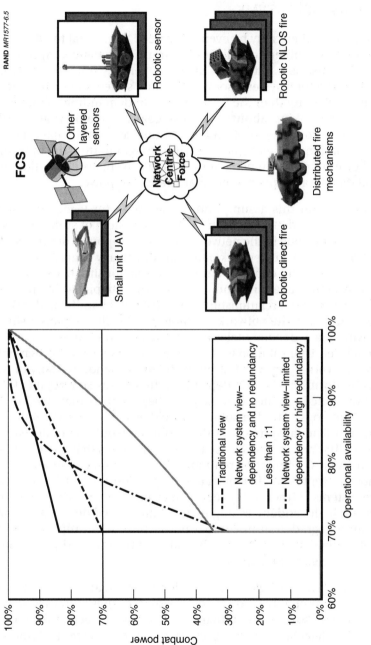

Figure 6.5—The Relationship Between A_o and Combat Power

A SYSTEM OF SYSTEMS

With the FCS, there may be even more need than usual to attack the sustainment problem on all fronts through a balanced approach. This is because as a system of systems, depending upon the network design of the total system, some individual systems may need even higher availability than the Army is used to demanding. Traditionally, when thinking about readiness goals, it seems that people assume that combat power and operational availability have a one-to-one relationship, as depicted by the straight dotted line in Figure 6.5. For example, if 70 percent of the tanks were available, the unit would then be at 70 percent combat strength or power.

Whether or not this assumption makes sense for legacy forces, it almost certainly does not for the FCS. As a system of systems, it is a network. One node in the network, depending upon its design, could shut down the entire network or at least drastically degrade its capabilities. Thus there could be a nonlinear relationship between individual system availability and combat power (depicted by the gray line) because of the relationship between all of the individual system availabilities and the network availability. This line depicts a situation with heavy dependencies and limited or no redundancy at the system level. One solution is to provide redundancy for the elements of the network upon which other elements depend. If many of the firing platforms in the FCS depend on the various sensors on UAVs and unmanned ground vehicles, then these sensors may need to be more numerous. Another solution would be to increase the pulse A_o of such individual systems. A third solution would be to develop a network that minimizes the use of "central" nodes that create strong dependencies. Similar to redundancy, this tactic can enable total combat power to remain almost unchanged despite the loss of one or more systems. Either heavy redundancy or a system that minimizes single node dependencies might create the curved dotted line, with very little degradation in combat power for initial drops in operational availability, which could be followed by a steep drop in combat power (e.g., as backups fail).

Since legacy forces fight as a combined arms team, the nonlinear relationship probably holds to some extent for these forces too. For example, tanks will have difficulty in successfully accomplishing a deliberate defense in open desert terrain if they have no Armored

Combat Earthmovers (ACEs) or bulldozers to dig fighting positions. On the other hand, there could be cases where the relationship is less than one to one, as depicted by the solid black line. This could occur in missions in which a unit's ability to accomplish the mission is based more on having a functioning maneuver element than on the number of operational systems.

PUTTING THE FCS PROGRAM IN CONTEXT

The last few examples suggest that the Army should pursue aggressive improvement and innovation in all means of keeping equipment available, because it would be risky to rely on just one to reach the very high pulse A_0 likely needed by the FCS, with the added difficulty of having to sustain equipment in the very demanding Objective Force operating environment envisioned. In terms of where the FCS is currently in the acquisition process, the Army should be exploring the feasible bounds of these categories as well as the costs and risks associated with the edges of the feasible region. In fact, through this type of tradespace exploration, many in the Army are realizing the potential inherent in each of the sustainment levers. They have realized that this type of approach will probably be more effective than relying on reliability alone. Increasingly, attention is being focused more broadly on availability and maintenance footprint with a recognition that reliability, maintainability, fleet life cycle management, and supply performance must all improve substantially to reach overall FCS goals. Further, draft unit designs now have a small number of maintainers combined with an expectation that maintainability improvements will enable significant crew-level repair capabilities.

Chapter Seven

CONCLUSION

The Army's Objective Force is seemingly about radical new operational concepts. However, none of the individual conceptual pieces are really new. What is new is the aggressiveness of the broad application of old principles and techniques, such as surprise and vertical maneuver, and the technology to take them to unprecedented heights. Similarly, the aggressiveness of the operational concepts and the resulting daunting demands on the logistics system at first create a feeling that something new must be developed to achieve the goals. However, nothing new, whether a design practice, a technology, or a sustainment concept, has been discussed in this report. What might be considered new is the need to apply the entire spectrum of tools for improving equipment sustainability. The tools exist; the issue is how effectively they are used. This requires a broad understanding across the Army of what it is trying to achieve and what tools are available. To that end, this report offers a number of recommendations.

DEVELOP AND BROADLY DISSEMINATE A FULL-SPECTRUM EQUIPMENT SUSTAINMENT REQUIREMENTS TEMPLATE

A standard set of metrics that addresses the full spectrum of equipment sustainment overall goals and design objectives should be developed and institutionalized. It should be well understood by each potential materiel solution proponency in the Army through incorporation into training, official guidance, and pamphlets. TRADOC's Combat Developments Engineering would employ it as the starting point in requirements development, which would ensure consideration in every program. The template would provide a standard framework for success and help align all Army materiel programs with CSS Transformation goals. The template should be viewed as a living document. As new sustainability concepts, better methods for defining requirements, or better metrics for measuring performance are developed, the template should be updated. Combat Developments Engineering, the functional directorates of Combat Developments, and the Army's program management offices should stay vigilant to capture new commercial practices, academic theories, or technologies that can be applied.

This report proposes an initial template of equipment sustainment requirements and associated metrics composed of two tiers. The first tier focuses on high-level equipment sustainment goals directly tied to Objective Force operational concepts and Army Transformation goals. They include operational availability during combat pulses—pulse A_o, maintenance footprint, pulse self-sufficiency, and total life cycle cost. Providing operational equipment, when needed, is the maintenance-oriented sustainment role in generating combat power. Providing this sustainment introduces two costs: maintenance footprint and maintenance cost. Pulse self-sufficiency limits the means for maintaining and generating operational equipment in a way consistent with Objective Force operational concepts.

Together, these four high-level type requirements bound the development of program sustainment concepts. As long as the targets for each are achieved, it does not matter to the operator on the ground or the Army leadership how they are achieved; their goals will have been met. Within a program, the high-level requirements will be useful for identifying potential tradeoffs and identifying sets of concepts that will enable the Army to transform.

The second tier of functional design requirements, derived from the targets for the overall goals, will help ensure that programs achieve intended results, and their presence in the template should help inform developers of potential paths to desired equipment sustainment performance. The identified potential generic functional design requirements are categorized into reliability, maintainability, fleet life cycle management, and supply support.

Reliability requirements reflect the effect of reliability on mission effectiveness and on total resource consumption. These are traditional Army requirements. Potential requirements in the template for the other three categories are much less traditional, although they are generally not entirely new to the Army.

While maintainability requirements are traditionally employed, the view of maintainability is sometimes too narrow. Maintainability requirements should consider the influence of design on downtime during operational pulses through three approaches: shorter wrench-turning time, more effective diagnostics, and the ability to anticipate and prevent failures during operational pulses through prognostics, preventive maintenance, and scheduled services. Workload requirements should reflect both the total amount as well as the distribution. More-maintainable systems that enable crews or operators to conduct a high proportion of maintenance could be a powerful lever for reducing footprint, generating self-sufficiency, reducing cost, and achieving desired pulse A_o.

Fleet life cycle management requirements represent a major gap in current requirements planning. Full treatment of these requirements should ensure that reliability degradation from system aging is considered, and it could force recognition of the need for either planned recapitalization programs or aggressive overhaul/phase maintenance regimes.

Supply support requirements are often excluded as well. However, stockage effectiveness requirements at each echelon of inventory could be set, and part and end item commonality goals could be formalized. Other supply support aspects could be considered on a limited base, depending upon program scope.

Establishing a "living" template can be an important tool in driving the Army's Transformation. As methods for achieving the overall goals become identified as desired solutions, the Army can, where it makes sense, drive their adoption through consistent emphasis in new programs. To do this, these methods should be reflected in requirements. Examples might include increased crew maintenance through appropriate designs, prognostics, and improved overhaul planning.

EXPAND THE USE OF REQUIREMENTS TO INTERNAL DoD PROVIDERS

Traditionally, requirements have been developed to serve as the basis of contractual specifications for systems developers. Thus, they have been externally focused. It is clear, though, that some of the template categories and requirements often fall under the responsibility of internal DoD providers. Instead of only being the basis for contractual specifications, requirements could also form the basis of performance agreements accepted by organizational commanders. The resources to meet these performance agreements would be a necessary condition for achieving the performance targets. This would have the added benefit of helping to increase the visibility of support funding, such as for initial spare parts provisioning, and associated performance shortfalls.

Under this paradigm, high-level requirements would be the responsibility of the program, not any one provider. The program would have to ensure that each provider does its part to allow the program to meet its overall goals. Alternatively, the high-level goals could form the basis of contractor requirements for programs that want to pursue extensive contractor logistics support concepts.

ENSURE THAT REASONABLE ASSUMPTIONS ALWAYS FORM THE BASIS FOR REQUIREMENTS

A critical element in ensuring that all of the overall requirements are actually achieved when requirements are met is the use of good assumptions in the requirements determination process. Functional requirements are often derived from overall goals using a series of assumptions. When the assumptions are not accurate, they will lead to requirements that will not produce desired outcomes. To the extent that assumptions drive program requirements, they should be made into requirements. An example would be the spare parts investment. ALDT assumptions at their heart rest on three sub-assumptions: the local inventory fill rate, distribution performance, and the wholesale fill rate. If any of these are assumed to be different than status quo levels, such as local stockage effectiveness, then the difference should be justified, reflected as a requirement, and resourced.

Whenever requirements are presented, the major assumptions should be shown at the same time. It is then up to the CSS community to ensure their validity. In some respects, one might think of this as akin to full financial disclosure for corporations. For investors to appreciate fully the value and risks of an investment, they want to be sure they understand a company's financial picture, including any relevant assumptions.

HIGH-LEVEL SUSTAINABILITY REQUIREMENTS MERIT CONSIDERATION AS KPPs

The high-level sustainability requirements should be reviewed by the Army to assess their desirability as KPPs. These requirements do not necessarily have to be limited to maintenance sustainment; they could potentially include all sustainment requirements. The broad equipment sustainment requirement categories found desirable as potential KPPs should be further developed to identify good metrics that can be reliably assessed.

ADOPT A BROAD SPECTRUM OF NON-KPP INITIATIVES FOR MOTIVATING EQUIPMENT SUSTAINMENT IMPROVEMENT

Beyond the option of designating one or more equipment sustainment requirements as KPPs, the Army should explore the potential value of greater use of additional policies and strategies for driving improved equipment sustainment performance. Such policies and strategies could be of two types: those designed to foster maximum possible performance, and those designed to increase process discipline (short of a KPP) to ensure that threshold requirements are achieved. They include the treatment of sustainment requirements as milestone exit criteria, equipment sustainment as a mandatory briefing topic in such forums as the Army Requirements Oversight Council and milestone decision reviews, the inclusion of sustainment requirements as critical operational issues and criteria, resourcing testing to enable reliability growth and maturation during the development process, providing financial incentives for achieving equipment sustainment goals (above thresholds), and increasing the emphasis on contractor past performance and product development management practices in contractor selection.

APPLY ALL OF THE EQUIPMENT SUSTAINMENT LEVERS IN TANDEM

The Army will need to pursue improvements and innovations across all means of keeping equipment available, because the gap between current and desired capabilities is quite substantial. Demand for maintenance resources during operational pulses should be reduced through better reliability, easier-to-repair systems, improved diagnostics, improved ability to prevent failures from occurring during combat pulses, and enhanced training. Maintenance, during and between pulses, should be facilitated by relatively robust spare parts support facilitated by platform commonality and distribution-based logistics (this does not mean a lot of spare parts, it just means good performance). Performance degradation and the resulting need for recapitalization to maintain capabilities over a system's life cycle should be treated up front and included in a comprehensive assessment of life cycle costs. The aforementioned metrics facilitate the ability for requirements developers to consider all of these elements of the equipment sustainment tradespace and how they interact to produce equipment availability, maintenance footprint, and cost.

ESTIMATING PULSE A_0

Figure A.1 provides additional detail on potential sources and methods for generating parameter estimates. At a high level, pulse A_0 should be developed from a simulation.

The simulation's data requirements should be developed through empirical data analysis, closed-form modeling, physical testing, and embedded simulations, as appropriate for each data element and each weapon system program. Stockage and distribution data can be based to a great degree on empirical data analyses. To support this, CWT and stockage performance data are now available Army-wide through the ILAP, and EDA data are expected to become available in FY 2002, first in enhanced ILAP and then as part of the Global Combat Support System—Army Management module. The EDA will be useful in estimating how workaround rates change as the intensity of the situation changes. An embedded job shop-type simulation could be used to produce maintenance shop time estimates (peacetime maintenance shop time estimates are likely to be poor predictors of wartime performance because of differences in available productive maintenance hours per maintainer). Testing should continue to produce reliability estimates, although advances in computing technology should enable a gradual migration of some portion of reliability analyses to simulation.

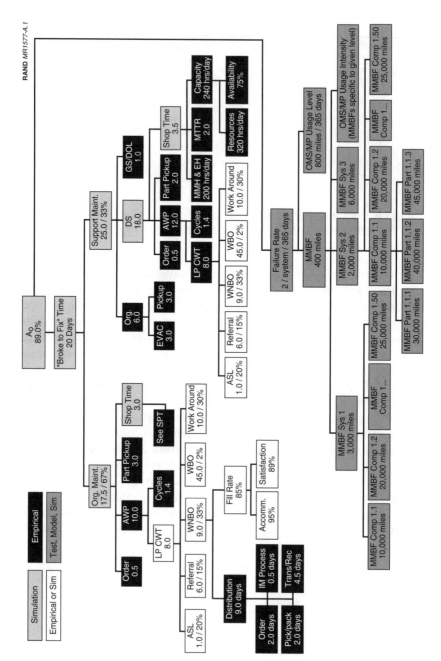

Figure A.1—Sources for A_o Parameter Estimates

MOS TO CATEGORY MAPPINGS

Enl/Off/WO and **MOS**	**Branch/Function**	**Category**
E11B	Infantry	Combat Arms
E11C	Infantry	Combat Arms
E11H	Infantry	Combat Arms
E11M	Infantry	Combat Arms
E11Z	Infantry	Combat Arms
E12B	Combat Engineering	Combat Support
E12C	Combat Engineering	Combat Support
E12Z	Combat Engineering	Combat Support
E13B	Field Artillery	Combat Arms
E13C	Field Artillery	Combat Arms
E13D	Field Artillery	Combat Arms
E13E	Field Artillery	Combat Arms
E13F	Field Artillery	Combat Arms
E13M	Field Artillery	Combat Arms
E13P	Field Artillery	Combat Arms
E13R	Field Artillery	Combat Arms
E13Z	Field Artillery	Combat Arms
E82C	Field Artillery	Combat Arms
E93F	Field Artillery	Combat Arms
E14D	Air Defense Artillery	Combat Arms
E14E	Air Defense Artillery	Combat Arms
E14J	Air Defense Artillery	Combat Arms
E14L	Air Defense Artillery	Combat Arms

E14M	Air Defense Artillery	Combat Arms
E14R	Air Defense Artillery	Combat Arms
E14S	Air Defense Artillery	Combat Arms
E14T	Air Defense Artillery	Combat Arms
E14Z	Air Defense Artillery	Combat Arms
E23R	Air Defense Artillery	Combat Arms
E18B	Special Forces	Combat Arms
E18C	Special Forces	Combat Arms
E18D	Special Forces	Combat Arms
E18E	Special Forces	Combat Arms
E18F	Special Forces	Combat Arms
E18Z	Special Forces	Combat Arms
E19D	Armor	Combat Arms
E19K	Armor	Combat Arms
E19Z	Armor	Combat Arms
E25M	Visual Information	Combat Service Support
E25R	Visual Information	Combat Service Support
E25V	Visual Information	Combat Service Support
E25Z	Visual Information	Combat Service Support
E31C	Signal Operations	Combat Support
E31F	Signal Operations	Combat Support
E31L	Signal Operations	Combat Support
E31P	Signal Operations	Combat Support
E31R	Signal Operations	Combat Support
E31S	Signal Operations	Combat Support
E31T	Signal Operations	Combat Support
E31U	Signal Operations	Combat Support
E31W	Signal Operations	Combat Support
E31Z	Signal Operations	Combat Support
E33W	Signal Operations	Combat Support
E27E	Electronic Maintenance and Calibration	Maintenance
E27G	Electronic Maintenance and Calibration	Maintenance
E27M	Electronic Maintenance and Calibration	Maintenance
E27T	Electronic Maintenance and Calibration	Maintenance
E27X	Electronic Maintenance and Calibration	Maintenance
E27Z	Electronic Maintenance and Calibration	Maintenance
E35D	Electronic Maintenance and Calibration	Maintenance

E35E	Electronic Maintenance and Calibration	Maintenance
E35F	Electronic Maintenance and Calibration	Maintenance
E35H	Electronic Maintenance and Calibration	Maintenance
E35J	Electronic Maintenance and Calibration	Maintenance
E35L	Electronic Maintenance and Calibration	Maintenance
E35M	Electronic Maintenance and Calibration	Maintenance
E35N	Electronic Maintenance and Calibration	Maintenance
E35R	Electronic Maintenance and Calibration	Maintenance
E35W	Electronic Maintenance and Calibration	Maintenance
E35Y	Electronic Maintenance and Calibration	Maintenance
E35Z	Electronic Maintenance and Calibration	Maintenance
E39B	Electronic Maintenance and Calibration	Maintenance
E37F	Psychological Operations	Combat Service Support
E38A	Civil Affairs	Combat Service Support
E46Q	Public Affairs	Combat Service Support
E46R	Public Affairs	Combat Service Support
E46Z	Public Affairs	Combat Service Support
E00B	General Engineering	Combat Support
E51B	General Engineering	Combat Support
E51H	General Engineering	Combat Support
E51K	General Engineering	Combat Support
E51M	General Engineering	Combat Support
E51R	General Engineering	Combat Support
E51T	General Engineering	Combat Support
E51Z	General Engineering	Combat Support
E52E	General Engineering	Combat Support
E52G	General Engineering	Combat Support
E62E	General Engineering	Combat Support
E62F	General Engineering	Combat Support
E62G	General Engineering	Combat Support
E62H	General Engineering	Combat Support
E62J	General Engineering	Combat Support
E62N	General Engineering	Combat Support
E54B	Chemical	Combat Support
E55B	Ammunition	Combat Service Support
E55D	EOD	Combat Service Support
E44B	Mechanical Maintenance	Maintenance

E44E	Mechanical Maintenance	Maintenance
E45B	Mechanical Maintenance	Maintenance
E45D	Mechanical Maintenance	Maintenance
E45E	Mechanical Maintenance	Maintenance
E45G	Mechanical Maintenance	Maintenance
E45K	Mechanical Maintenance	Maintenance
E45N	Mechanical Maintenance	Maintenance
E45T	Mechanical Maintenance	Maintenance
E52C	Mechanical Maintenance	Maintenance
E52D	Mechanical Maintenance	Maintenance
E52X	Mechanical Maintenance	Maintenance
E62B	Mechanical Maintenance	Maintenance
E63A	Mechanical Maintenance	Maintenance
E63B	Mechanical Maintenance	Maintenance
E63D	Mechanical Maintenance	Maintenance
E63E	Mechanical Maintenance	Maintenance
E63G	Mechanical Maintenance	Maintenance
E63H	Mechanical Maintenance	Maintenance
E63J	Mechanical Maintenance	Maintenance
E63M	Mechanical Maintenance	Maintenance
E63N	Mechanical Maintenance	Maintenance
E63S	Mechanical Maintenance	Maintenance
E63T	Mechanical Maintenance	Maintenance
E63W	Mechanical Maintenance	Maintenance
E63Y	Mechanical Maintenance	Maintenance
E63Z	Mechanical Maintenance	Maintenance
E67G	Mechanical Maintenance	Maintenance
E67N	Mechanical Maintenance	Maintenance
E67R	Mechanical Maintenance	Maintenance
E67S	Mechanical Maintenance	Maintenance
E67T	Mechanical Maintenance	Maintenance
E67U	Mechanical Maintenance	Maintenance
E67V	Mechanical Maintenance	Maintenance
E67Y	Mechanical Maintenance	Maintenance
E67Z	Mechanical Maintenance	Maintenance
E68B	Mechanical Maintenance	Maintenance
E68D	Mechanical Maintenance	Maintenance

E68F	Mechanical Maintenance	Maintenance
E68G	Mechanical Maintenance	Maintenance
E68H	Mechanical Maintenance	Maintenance
E68J	Mechanical Maintenance	Maintenance
E68K	Mechanical Maintenance	Maintenance
E68N	Mechanical Maintenance	Maintenance
E68S	Mechanical Maintenance	Maintenance
E68X	Mechanical Maintenance	Maintenance
E68Y	Mechanical Maintenance	Maintenance
E71D	Administration	Combat Service Support
E71L	Administration	Combat Service Support
E71M	Administration	Combat Service Support
E73C	Administration	Combat Service Support
E73D	Administration	Combat Service Support
E73Z	Administration	Combat Service Support
E75B	Administration	Combat Service Support
E75F	Administration	Combat Service Support
E75H	Administration	Combat Service Support
E74B	Information Systems Operations	Combat Service Support
E74C	Information Systems Operations	Combat Service Support
E74Z	Information Systems Operations	Combat Service Support
E77F	Petroleum and Water	Combat Service Support
E77L	Petroleum and Water	Combat Service Support
E77W	Petroleum and Water	Combat Service Support
E79R	Recruiting and Retention	Combat Service Support
E79S	Recruiting and Retention	Combat Service Support
E79T	Recruiting and Retention	Combat Service Support
E79V	Recruiting and Retention	Combat Service Support
E81L	Topographic Engineering	Combat Support
E81T	Topographic Engineering	Combat Support
E81Z	Topographic Engineering	Combat Support
E82D	Topographic Engineering	Combat Support
E88H	Transportation	Combat Service Support
E88K	Transportation	Combat Service Support
E88L	Transportation	Combat Service Support
E88M	Transportation	Combat Service Support
E88N	Transportation	Combat Service Support

E88P	Transportation	Combat Service Support
E88T	Transportation	Combat Service Support
E88U	Transportation	Combat Service Support
E88X	Transportation	Combat Service Support
E88Z	Transportation	Combat Service Support
E91A	Medical	Combat Service Support
E91D	Medical	Combat Service Support
E91E	Medical	Combat Service Support
E91G	Medical	Combat Service Support
E91H	Medical	Combat Service Support
E91J	Medical	Combat Service Support
E91K	Medical	Combat Service Support
E91M	Medical	Combat Service Support
E91P	Medical	Combat Service Support
E91Q	Medical	Combat Service Support
E91R	Medical	Combat Service Support
E91S	Medical	Combat Service Support
E91T	Medical	Combat Service Support
E91V	Medical	Combat Service Support
E91W	Medical	Combat Service Support
E91X	Medical	Combat Service Support
E91Z	Medical	Combat Service Support
E43M	Supply and Services	Combat Service Support
E57E	Supply and Services	Combat Service Support
E92A	Supply and Services	Combat Service Support
E92G	Supply and Services	Combat Service Support
E92M	Supply and Services	Combat Service Support
E92R	Supply and Services	Combat Service Support
E92Y	Supply and Services	Combat Service Support
E92Z	Supply and Services	Combat Service Support
E93C	Aviation Operations	Combat Support
E93P	Aviation Operations	Combat Support
E95B	Military Police	Combat Support
E95C	Military Police	Combat Support
E95D	Military Police	Combat Support
E96B	Military Intelligence	Combat Support
E96D	Military Intelligence	Combat Support

E96H	Military Intelligence	Combat Support
E96R	Military Intelligence	Combat Support
E96U	Military Intelligence	Combat Support
E96Z	Military Intelligence	Combat Support
E97B	Military Intelligence	Combat Support
E97E	Military Intelligence	Combat Support
E97L	Military Intelligence	Combat Support
E97Z	Military Intelligence	Combat Support
E02B	Bands	Combat Service Support
E02C	Bands	Combat Service Support
E02D	Bands	Combat Service Support
E02E	Bands	Combat Service Support
E02F	Bands	Combat Service Support
E02G	Bands	Combat Service Support
E02H	Bands	Combat Service Support
E02J	Bands	Combat Service Support
E02K	Bands	Combat Service Support
E02L	Bands	Combat Service Support
E02M	Bands	Combat Service Support
E02N	Bands	Combat Service Support
E02S	Bands	Combat Service Support
E02T	Bands	Combat Service Support
E02U	Bands	Combat Service Support
E02Z	Bands	Combat Service Support
E98C	Signals Intelligence/Electronic Warfare Ops	Combat Support
E98G	Signals Intelligence/Electronic Warfare Ops	Combat Support
E98H	Signals Intelligence/Electronic Warfare Ops	Combat Support
E98J	Signals Intelligence/Electronic Warfare Ops	Combat Support
E98K	Signals Intelligence/Electronic Warfare Ops	Combat Support
E98Z	Signals Intelligence/Electronic Warfare Ops	Combat Support
O11A	Infantry	Combat Arms
O12A	Armor	Combat Arms
O12B	Armor	Combat Arms
O12C	Armor	Combat Arms
O13A	Field Artillery	Combat Arms
O14A	Air Defense Artillery	Combat Arms
O14B	Air Defense Artillery	Combat Arms

O14D	Air Defense Artillery	Combat Arms
O14E	Air Defense Artillery	Combat Arms
O15A	Aviation CS	Combat Support
O15B	Aviation	Combat Arms
O15C	Aviation CS	Combat Support
O15D	Aviation Logistics	Combat Service Support
O18A	Special Forces	Combat Arms
O21A	Engineers	Combat Support
O21B	Engineers	Combat Support
O21D	Engineers	Combat Support
O25A	Signal Corps	Combat Support
O31A	Military Police	Combat Support
O35B	Military Intelligence	Combat Support
O35C	Military Intelligence	Combat Support
O35D	Military Intelligence	Combat Support
O35E	Military Intelligence	Combat Support
O35F	Military Intelligence	Combat Support
O35G	Military Intelligence	Combat Support
O38A	Civil Affairs	Combat Service Support
O42B	Adjutant General	Combat Service Support
O42C	Adjutant General	Combat Service Support
O44A	Finance	Combat Service Support
O55A	Judge Advocate General	Combat Service Support
O55B	Judge Advocate General	Combat Service Support
O56A	Chaplain	Combat Service Support
O56D	Chaplain	Combat Service Support
O60A	Medical Corps	Combat Service Support
O60B	Medical Corps	Combat Service Support
O60C	Medical Corps	Combat Service Support
O60D	Medical Corps	Combat Service Support
O60F	Medical Corps	Combat Service Support
O60G	Medical Corps	Combat Service Support
O60H	Medical Corps	Combat Service Support
O60J	Medical Corps	Combat Service Support
O60K	Medical Corps	Combat Service Support
O60L	Medical Corps	Combat Service Support
O60M	Medical Corps	Combat Service Support

O60N	Medical Corps	Combat Service Support
O60P	Medical Corps	Combat Service Support
O60Q	Medical Corps	Combat Service Support
O60R	Medical Corps	Combat Service Support
O60S	Medical Corps	Combat Service Support
O60T	Medical Corps	Combat Service Support
O60U	Medical Corps	Combat Service Support
O60V	Medical Corps	Combat Service Support
O60W	Medical Corps	Combat Service Support
O61A	Medical Corps	Combat Service Support
O61B	Medical Corps	Combat Service Support
O61C	Medical Corps	Combat Service Support
O61D	Medical Corps	Combat Service Support
O61E	Medical Corps	Combat Service Support
O61F	Medical Corps	Combat Service Support
O61G	Medical Corps	Combat Service Support
O61H	Medical Corps	Combat Service Support
O61J	Medical Corps	Combat Service Support
O61K	Medical Corps	Combat Service Support
O61L	Medical Corps	Combat Service Support
O61M	Medical Corps	Combat Service Support
O61N	Medical Corps	Combat Service Support
O61P	Medical Corps	Combat Service Support
O61Q	Medical Corps	Combat Service Support
O61R	Medical Corps	Combat Service Support
O61U	Medical Corps	Combat Service Support
O61W	Medical Corps	Combat Service Support
O61Z	Medical Corps	Combat Service Support
O62A	Medical Corps	Combat Service Support
O62B	Medical Corps	Combat Service Support
O63A	Dental Corps	Combat Service Support
O63B	Dental Corps	Combat Service Support
O63D	Dental Corps	Combat Service Support
O63E	Dental Corps	Combat Service Support
O63F	Dental Corps	Combat Service Support
O63H	Dental Corps	Combat Service Support
O63K	Dental Corps	Combat Service Support

O63M	Dental Corps	Combat Service Support
O63N	Dental Corps	Combat Service Support
O63P	Dental Corps	Combat Service Support
O63R	Dental Corps	Combat Service Support
O64A	Veterinary Corps	Combat Service Support
O64B	Veterinary Corps	Combat Service Support
O64C	Veterinary Corps	Combat Service Support
O64D	Veterinary Corps	Combat Service Support
O64E	Veterinary Corps	Combat Service Support
O64F	Veterinary Corps	Combat Service Support
O64Z	Veterinary Corps	Combat Service Support
O65A	Army Medical Specialist	Combat Service Support
O65B	Army Medical Specialist	Combat Service Support
O65C	Army Medical Specialist	Combat Service Support
O65D	Army Medical Specialist	Combat Service Support
O66C	Nurse	Combat Service Support
O66E	Nurse	Combat Service Support
O66F	Nurse	Combat Service Support
O66H	Nurse	Combat Service Support
O66N	Nurse	Combat Service Support
O67A	Medical Service	Combat Service Support
O67B	Medical Service	Combat Service Support
O67C	Medical Service	Combat Service Support
O67D	Medical Service	Combat Service Support
O67E	Medical Service	Combat Service Support
O67F	Medical Service	Combat Service Support
O67G	Medical Service	Combat Service Support
O67J	Medical Service	Combat Service Support
O74A	Chemical	Combat Support
O74B	Chemical	Combat Support
O74C	Chemical	Combat Support
O88A	Transportation	Combat Service Support
O88B	Transportation	Combat Service Support
O88C	Transportation	Combat Service Support
O88D	Transportation	Combat Service Support
O91A	Ordnance	Maintenance
O91B	Ordnance	Maintenance

O91D	Ordnance	Maintenance
O91E	Ordnance	Maintenance
O92A	Quartermaster	Combat Service Support
O92D	Quartermaster	Combat Service Support
O92F	Quartermaster	Combat Service Support
O24A	Information Systems Eng	Combat Service Support
O24B	Information Systems Eng	Combat Service Support
O24Z	Information Systems Eng	Combat Service Support
O30A	Information Operations	Combat Service Support
O34A	Strategic Intelligence	Combat Support
O39A	PSYOPS and Civil Affairs	Combat Service Support
O39B	PSYOPS and Civil Affairs	Combat Service Support
O39C	PSYOPS and Civil Affairs	Combat Service Support
O39X	PSYOPS and Civil Affairs	Combat Service Support
O40A	Space Operations	Combat Service Support
O43A	Human Resource Management	Combat Service Support
O45A	Comptroller	Combat Service Support
O46A	Public Affairs	Combat Service Support
O46B	Public Affairs	Combat Service Support
O46X	Public Affairs	Combat Service Support
O47A	U.S. Military Academy	Other
O47C	U.S. Military Academy	Other
O47D	U.S. Military Academy	Other
O47F	U.S. Military Academy	Other
O47G	U.S. Military Academy	Other
O47H	U.S. Military Academy	Other
O47J	U.S. Military Academy	Other
O47K	U.S. Military Academy	Other
O47L	U.S. Military Academy	Other
O47M	U.S. Military Academy	Other
O47N	U.S. Military Academy	Other
O47P	U.S. Military Academy	Other
O47Q	U.S. Military Academy	Other
O47R	U.S. Military Academy	Other
O47S	U.S. Military Academy	Other
O48B	Foreign Area Office	Combat Service Support
O48C	Foreign Area Office	Combat Service Support

O48D	Foreign Area Office	Combat Service Support
O48E	Foreign Area Office	Combat Service Support
O48F	Foreign Area Office	Combat Service Support
O48G	Foreign Area Office	Combat Service Support
O48H	Foreign Area Office	Combat Service Support
O48I	Foreign Area Office	Combat Service Support
O48J	Foreign Area Office	Combat Service Support
O48X	Foreign Area Office	Combat Service Support
O49A	ORSA	Combat Service Support
O49W	ORSA	Combat Service Support
O49X	ORSA	Combat Service Support
O50A	Force Development	Combat Service Support
O51A	Acquisition	Combat Service Support
O51C	Acquisition	Combat Service Support
O51R	Acquisition	Combat Service Support
O51S	Acquisition	Combat Service Support
O51T	Acquisition	Combat Service Support
O51Z	Acquisition	Combat Service Support
O52B	Nuclear Research and Operations	Combat Support
O53A	Information Systems Management	Combat Service Support
O53X	Information Systems Management	Combat Service Support
O57A	Simulations	Combat Service Support
O59A	Strategic Plans	Combat Service Support
O90A	Logistics	Combat Service Support
O70A	Health Services	Combat Service Support
O70B	Health Services	Combat Service Support
O70C	Health Services	Combat Service Support
O70D	Health Services	Combat Service Support
O70E	Health Services	Combat Service Support
O70F	Health Services	Combat Service Support
O70H	Health Services	Combat Service Support
O70K	Health Services	Combat Service Support
O71A	Laboratory Sciences	Combat Service Support
O71B	Laboratory Sciences	Combat Service Support
O71E	Laboratory Sciences	Combat Service Support
O71F	Laboratory Sciences	Combat Service Support
O72A	Preventive Medicine	Combat Service Support

O72B	Preventive Medicine	Combat Service Support
O72C	Preventive Medicine	Combat Service Support
O72D	Preventive Medicine	Combat Service Support
O72E	Preventive Medicine	Combat Service Support
O73A	Behavioral Sciences	Combat Service Support
O73B	Behavioral Sciences	Combat Service Support
O01A	Immaterial	Other
O02A	Immaterial	Combat Arms
O05A	Immaterial	Combat Service Support
O00A	Reporting	Other
O00B	General	Combat Arms
O00C	Reporting	Other
O00D	Reporting	Other
O00E	Reporting	Other
W131A	Field Artillery	Combat Arms
W140A	Air Defense Artillery	Combat Arms
W140B	Air Defense Artillery	Combat Arms
W140D	Air Defense Artillery	Combat Arms
W140E	Air Defense Artillery	Combat Arms
W150A	Aviation Operations	Combat Support
W151A	Aviation Maintenance	Maintenance
W152B	Aviation Combat	Combat Arms
W152C	Aviation Combat	Combat Arms
W152D	Aviation Combat	Combat Arms
W152F	Aviation Combat	Combat Arms
W152G	Aviation Combat	Combat Arms
W152H	Aviation Combat	Combat Arms
W153A	Aviation CS	Combat Support
W153B	Aviation CS	Combat Support
W153D	Aviation CS	Combat Support
W153E	Aviation CS	Combat Support
W154C	Aviation CSS	Combat Service Support
W154E	Aviation CSS	Combat Service Support
W155A	Aviation CS	Combat Support
W155E	Aviation CSS	Combat Service Support
W155F	Aviation CSS	Combat Service Support
W155G	Aviation CS	Combat Support

W180A	Special Forces	Combat Arms
W210A	Engineers	Combat Support
W215D	Engineers	Combat Support
W250N	Signal Corps	Combat Support
W251A	Signal Corps	Combat Support
W311A	Military Police	Combat Support
W350B	Military Intelligence	Combat Support
W350D	Military Intelligence	Combat Support
W350L	Military Intelligence	Combat Support
W351B	Military Intelligence	Combat Support
W351C	Military Intelligence	Combat Support
W351E	Military Intelligence	Combat Support
W352C	Military Intelligence	Combat Support
W352G	Military Intelligence	Combat Support
W352H	Military Intelligence	Combat Support
W352J	Military Intelligence	Combat Support
W352K	Military Intelligence	Combat Support
W353A	Military Intelligence	Combat Support
W420A	Adjutant General	Combat Service Support
W420C	Adjutant General	Combat Service Support
W550A	Judge Advocate General	Combat Service Support
W600A	Medical Corps	Combat Service Support
W640A	Veterinary	Combat Service Support
W670A	Medical Service	Combat Service Support
W880A	Transportation	Combat Service Support
W881A	Transportation	Combat Service Support
W882A	Transportation	Combat Service Support
W910A	Ammo	Combat Service Support
W913A	Ordnance	Maintenance
W914A	Ordnance	Maintenance
W915A	Ordnance	Maintenance
W915E	Ordnance	Maintenance
W918B	Ordnance	Maintenance
W918D	Ordnance	Maintenance
W918E	Ordnance	Maintenance
W919A	Ordnance	Maintenance
W920A	Quartermaster	Combat Service Support

W920B	Quartermaster	Combat Service Support
W921A	Quartermaster	Combat Service Support
W922A	Quartermaster	Combat Service Support

ESTIMATED ANNUAL COST OF MAINTENANCE

The following tables show how the costs of each maintenance category were estimated.

Maintenance Labor: Active Army 1999 Maintenance Personnel Inventory

Branch/CMF	E00	E01	E02	E03	E04	E05	E06	E07	E08	E09	Total
E29: Signal Maint						4	15	10	10	1	40
E33: Elec War/ Inter Sys Maint		109	88	104	263	155	195	98	37	8	1,057
E35: Elec Maint and Calibr		465	507	742	1,702	1,206	1,139	640	169	23	6,593
E63: Mech Maint		3,427	3,664	6,207	11,359	7,185	4,087	2,931	758	93	39,711
E67: Aircraft Maint		922	1,335	1,471	4,050	2,813	2,133	1,287	387	56	14,454
Total	0	4,923	5,594	8,524	17,374	11,363	7,569	4,966	1,361	181	61,855
DoD Comp Rate ($)		27,425	26,725	27,925	33,000	39,550	47,000	54,450	63,050	75,400	
Comp Rate Cost ($)		135,013,275	149,499,650	238,032,700	573,342,000	449,406,650	355,743,000	270,398,700	85,811,050	13,647,400	2,270,894,425

Branch/CMF	O00	O01	O02	O03	O04	O05	O06	O07	O08	O09	O10	Total
O91: Ordn Corps		366	472	913	630	340	148	8	5	1	1	2,884
Total	0	366	472	913	630	340	148	8	5	1	1	2,884
DoD Comp Rate ($)		45,050	58,925	77,900	94,025	111,650	133,900	144,175	156,900	170,175	165,250	
Comp Rate Cost ($)		16,488,300	27,812,600	71,122,700	59,235,750	37,961,000	19,817,200	1,153,400	784,500	170,175	165,250	234,710,875

Branch/CMF	W01	W02	W03	W04	W05	Total
W91: Ordnance	256	711	440	225	48	1,680
Total	256	711	440	225	48	1,680
DoD Comp Rate ($)	52,525	60,375	70,750	85,475	98,675	
Comp Rate Cost ($)	13,446,400	42,926,625	31,130,000	19,231,875	4,736,400	111,471,300

Total Maint Personnel	66,419
Total Maint Manpower Cost ($)	2,617,076,600

SOURCE: FORMIS, DMDC.

Maintenance Labor: Army National Guard 1999 Maintenance Personnel Inventory

Branch/CMF	Military Grade										
	E00	E01	E02	E03	E04	E05	E06	E07	E08	E09	Total
E23: Air Defense Sys Maint				2	10	7	1		0		20
E27: Land Cbt and ADA D/GS Spt Maint							1	1			2
E29: Signal Maint				1	4	3	2				10
E33: Elec War/Inter Sys Maint		1		2	17	7	3				30
E35: Elec Maint and Calibr		259	144	377	1,010	832	532	254	62	3	3,473
E63: Mechanical Maint		2,477	1,552	3,830	15,036	10,468	4,856	3,086	921	70	42,296
E67: Aircraft Maint		629	290	847	2,346	2,882	2,187	820	359	22	10,382
Total	0	3,366	1,986	5,059	18,423	14,199	7,582	4,161	1,342	95	56,213

Branch/CMF	O01	O02	O03	O04	O05	O06	O07	O08	Total	% Total WO
O91: Ordnance Corps	61	331	470	298	124	53	5	2	1,154	14.5%
Total	61	331	470	298	124	53	5	2	1,154	14.5%

Branch/CMF	W00	W01	W02	W03	W04	W05	Total
W91: Ordnance		94	449	234	348	29	1,154
Total	0	94	449	234	348	29	1,154

Total Maintenance Personnel   58,711

FY 2001 Army budget

1999 ARNG pay and benefits	$3,613,000,000
1999 ARNG personnel	357,000
Average cost per person	10,120

Total Cost, Guard Maintenance Personnel ; Average Cost @ $10,120/yr $594,155,320

SOURCE: FORMIS, DMDC.

Maintenance Labor: Army Reserve 1999 Maintenance Personnel Inventory

Branch/CMF	Military Grade									
	E01	E02	E03	E04	E05	E06	E07	E08	E09	Total
E23: Air Defense Sys Maint			2		1					13
E27: Land Cbt and ADA D/GS Spt Maint				3						3
E29: Signal Maint		1		9	4	1		5		20
E33: Elec War/Inter Sys Maint	1			11	4	5		1		24
E35: Elec Maint and Calibr	19	21	44	230	179	109	55	19	1	677
E63: Mechanical Maint	1,200	864	1,778	5,375	2,883	1,682	1,213	462	29	15,486
E67: Aircraft Maint	43	31	81	314	252	167	60	27	3	978
Total	1,263	917	1,905	5,952	3,323	1,964	1,330	514	33	17,201

Branch/CMF	O01	O02	O03	O04	O05	O06	O07	O08	O09	Total
O91: Ordnance Corps	52	259	549	441	220	32	0	0	1,553	1,553
Total	52	259	549	441	220	32	0	0	1,553	1,553

Branch/CMF	W00	W01	W02	W03	W04	W05	Total
W91: Ordnance	0	24	164	124	198	4	514
Total	0	24	164	124	198	4	514

Total Maintenance Personnel	19,268
FY 2001 Army budget	
1999 USAR pay and benefits	$2,179,000,000
1999 USAR personnel	207,000
Average cost per person	10,527
Total Cost, Reserve Maintenance Personnel; Average Cost @ $10,527/yr	$202,834,236

SOURCE: FORMIS, DMDC.

Maintenance Labor:
Army 1999 Non-AMC-Depot Civilian Personnel Inventory

Civilian Occupation	Total Assigned
8852: Aircraft Mechanic	2,456
8840: Aircraft Mechanical Parts Repair	310
8810: Aircraft Propeller Mechanic	74
8807: Aircraft Propeller/Rotor Mechanic	7
8610: Small Engine Mechanic	37
8602: Aircraft Engine Mechanic	215
8601: Misc Aircraft Engine Overhaul	0
8268: Aircraft Pneudraulic Sys Mechanic	109
8255: Pneudraulic Sys Mechanic	107
6656: Special Weapons Sys Mechanic	1
6652: Aircraft Ordnance Sys Mechanic	35
6601: Misc Armament Work	79
5876: Electromotive Equip Mechanic	11
5823: Automotive Mechanic	3,209
5803: Heavy Mobile Equip Mechanic	7,117
5439: Testing Equip Operating	22
5378: Powered Support Sys Mechanic	216
5334: Marine Machinery Mechanic	124
4818: Aircraft Survival & Flight Equip Repairer	101
4749: Maintenance Mechanic	2,123
4737: General Equip Mechanic	74
4704: Maintaining Supervising	0
3809: Mobile Equip Metal Mechanic	186
3725: Battery Repair	23
3359: Instrument Mechanic	107
3306: Optical Instrument Repair	125
2604: Electronics Mechanic	3,696
2602: Electronic Measurement Equip Mechanic	599
0856: Electronics Technician	1,038
Depot Maintenance WCF personnel costs (FY01 AWCF budget)	$ 657,000,000
Depot Maintenance WCF personnel (FY01 AWCF budget)	12,292
Cost per person	$ 53,449
Civilian maintenance personnel (FORMIS)	22,201
Depot maintenance personnel (Depot Maint Business Profile)	8,390
Nondepot civilian maintenance personnel	13,811
Estimated cost of nondepot maintenance personnel	$ 738,189,636

SOURCE: FORMIS, DMDC.

Supply Personnel: Active Army Requirement for MOS 92A Duty Positions Related to Spare Parts

Grade	E03	E04	E05	E06	E07	E08	Total	Average FY99 TTHS Personnel as % of Authorized	Total with Estimated TTHS
Number	1,429	2,977	3,244	401	164	30	8,245		
DoD Composite Rate	33,000	39,550	47,000	54,450	63,050	75,400			
Cost ($)	47,157,000	117,740,350	152,468,000	21,834,450	10,340,200	2,262,000	351,802,000	12.0%	394,018,240

Grade	O02	O03	O04	O05	Total				
Number	43	42	28	4	117				
DoD Composite Rate	58,925	77,900	94,025	111,650					
Cost ($)	2,533,775	3,271,800	2,632,700	446,600	8,884,875			17.5%	10,439,728

Grade	W02	W03	W04	W05	Total				
Number	124	32	16	3	175				
DoD Composite Rate	60,375	70,750	85,475	98,675					
Cost ($)	7,486,500	2,264,000	1,367,600	296,025	11,414,125			10.5%	12,612,608
								Total	417,070,576

Active Personnel Supply to Maintenance Cost Ratio	15.9%
Estimated USAR + ARNG maintenance cost	$796,989,559
Estimated USAR + ARNG supply personnel cost	$127,012,291

SOURCE: The Army Authorization Documents System, end of FY99. Quartermaster Personnel maintenance-related duty positions (authorized).

Non-AMC Maintenance Contracts

Command Category	Testing, Inspection, and Quality Control	Repair and Maintenance	Modification of Equipment	Technical Representative Service	Installation of Equipment	Total
AMC Acq	7,101,340	16,165,177	21,467,296	24,362,510		$69,096,323
AMCOM	4,281,701	47,861,962	2,627,430	80,206,631		$134,977,724
ARL		620,655		65,000		$685,655
Arsenals	577,106	3,911,151	39,200	67,000	1,950,908	$6,545,365
CECOM		122,600,363	114,860	47,569,299		$170,284,522
CENTCOM		64,260,033			35,260	$64,295,293
Depots		1,804,263		759,574		$2,563,837
EUSA		2,976,769			151,244	$3,128,013
FORSCOM		21,483,223		460,911	127,827	$22,071,961
INSCOM	201,935	8,070,492				$8,272,427
MTMC	99,556	3,380,584				$3,480,140
National Guard	155,073	2,077,770			100,863	$2,333,706
OPTEC						$0
Other						$0
PACOM		1,761,674		137,478	142,264	$2,041,416
Panama		863,182				$863,182
SBCCOM			42,500			$42,500
Signal and Info						$0
TACOM	637,777	27,191,505		2,717,215	–41,812	$30,504,685
TRADOC	174,225	124,655,789	56,768	480,474	176,695	$125,543,951
USAREUR	36,384	47,065,324	2,871,002	3,824,206	546,372	$54,343,288
USARSPACE		8,599,415				$8,599,415
USMA	198,732	5,147,839				$5,346,571
Total	$13,463,829	$510,497,170	$27,219,056	$160,650,298	$3,189,621	$715,019,974
Non-AMC	$ 865,905	$290,342,094		$ 4,903,069		$ 296,111,068
AMC	$ 12,597,924	$220,155,076		$155,747,229		$ 388,500,229

Procurement of Spare and Repair Parts for Initial Provisioning

Department of the Army 2001 Procurement Program, FY01 President's Budget Appropriation for spare and repair parts (1,000's)	
Other Procurement Army (OPA)	$ 58,994
Weapons/Tracked Combat Vehicles (WTCV)	$ 20,075
Missiles (MSLS)	$ 18,762
Aircraft (ACFT)	$ 27,486
Total	$ 125,317

Net OMA Spending to Supply Management, Army

Spare parts	$ 2,051,000,000
Other (DLA and GSA spares)	$ 687,000,000
Total	$ 2,738,000,000

SOURCE: AWCF Supply Management Army, FY99
Reapportionment Request.

Depot Maintenance Program

$ 621,500,000

SOURCE: FY 2001 OMA Budget.

OBJECTIVE TABLES OF
ORGANIZATION AND EQUIPMENT

87000F100, DIV XXI HVY DIV (AR) 4MECH, 28 August 1998

47100F300, IBCT, 18 May 2000

87000A700, AR DIV 1ST CAV, 28 August 1998

87100L100, HEAVY SEP BRIGADE (ARMOR), 03 June 1997

87100L200, HEAVY SEP BRIGADE (MECH), 03 June 1997

77000A000, LID (DOCTRINAL), 19 November 1998

63390F000, CBT SER SPT CO (CSSC) BSB, 06 September 2000

Interim Division (draft), 9 February 2001

LIST OF OPERATIONAL REQUIREMENTS DOCUMENTS REVIEWED

Defense Message System (DMS)—Army Service Extension into the Tactical Environment, CARDS 08045, 3 May 1999.

Department of the Army, Operational Requirements Document (ORD) for the Advanced Field Artillery System (AFAS) aka CRUSADER ORD 10 November 1994 0489.

Department of the Army, Operational Requirements Document (ORD) for the Advanced Precision Kill Weapon System (APKWS).

Department of the Army, Operational Requirements Document (ORD) for the AH-64A+ Apache Attack Helicopter ORD 19 August 1999 05014.

Department of the Army, Operational Requirements Document (ORD) for the Army Tactical Missile System (ATACMS) ORD 14 January 1999 0499.

Department of the Army, Operational Requirements Document (ORD) for the Bradley Linebacker, CARDS 0766, 5 September 1996.

Department of the Army, Operational Requirements Document (ORD) for the Breacher (Grizzley), 11 April 1996.

Department of the Army, Operational Requirements Document (ORD) for the Combat Service Support Control Systems (CSSCS), 08030, 9 April 1998.

Department of the Army, Operational Requirements Document (ORD) for the Containerized Chapel (CC) System, 14031, 12 October 1999.

Department of the Army, Operational Requirements Document (ORD) for the Containerized Maintenance Facility (CMF), 16076, December 1997.

Department of the Army, Operational Requirements Document (ORD) for the Containerized Kitchen (CK), 16061, 27 March 1998.

Department of the Army, Operational Requirements Document (ORD) for the Corps Surface-to-Air Missile (SAM) System ORD 05 October 1993 0760.

Department of the Army, Operational Requirements Document (ORD) for the Family of Interim Armored Vehicles (IAV) 22 February 2000.

Department of the Army, Operational Requirements Document (ORD) for the Forward Repair System (FRS), 16082.

Department of the Army, Operational Requirements Document (ORD) for the High Mobility Artillery Rocket System (HIMARS) ORD 19 October 1999 04003.

Department of the Army, Operational Requirements Document (ORD) for the Improved Medium Machine Gun (IMMG), CARDS 02044, August 1999.

Department of the Army, Operational Requirements Document (ORD) for the Joint Tactical Radio (JTR), 23 March 1998.

Department of the Army, Operational Requirements Document (ORD) for the Laundry Advanced System (LAS), 16051, 30 April 1997.

Department of the Army, Operational Requirements Document (ORD) for the M1A2 ORD 0379, 30 May 1994.

Department of the Army, Operational Requirements Document (ORD) for the M88A2, Heavy Equipment Recovery Combat Utility Lift and Evacuation System (HERCULES) Improved Recovery Vehicle, 0373, 9 November 1998.

Department of the Army, Operational Requirements Document (ORD) for the RAH-66, Comanche.

Department of the Army, Operational Requirements Document (ORD) for the Tactical Unmanned Aerial Vehicle (TUAV), CARDS 1583, 11 March 1999.

Department of the Army, Operational Requirements Document (ORD) for the Theater Logistics Vessel (TLV), 13 December 1999.

Department of the Army, Operational Requirements Document (ORD) for the Updated Required Operational Capability for a Rough Terrain Container Crane (RTCC), Cards Reference Number 1696, 16 January 1997.

EQUIPMENT SUSTAINMENT
REQUIREMENTS AND METRICS GUIDE

Mission Effectiveness (Availability of combat power)	This is the ultimate purpose of equipment sustainment.
Average Pulse Availability (Avg Pulse A_O)	Definition: Average percentage of a force that is mission capable over the course of a combat pulse. • Measures average level of combat power available during a combat pulse. • A function of maintenance footprint in the combat force, refit capability, pulse length and profile, mission-critical reliability (MTBSA), maintenance workload per failure (MMH/UMA–combat force), mean time to repair (MTTR), part wait time, recovery wait time, administrative/coordination delays, reliability degradation, prognostic capabilities, and preventive maintenance and scheduled service practices. • Should be looked at over a system's life cycle (MTBSA may change depending upon durability, overhaul, recapitalization, and planned replacements).
Minimum Pulse A_O (Min Pulse A_O)	Definition: The minimum level of availability (percentage of force that is mission capable) that a force is expected to maintain over the course of a combat pulse. • Measures the minimum expected level of combat power that will be available over the course of a combat pulse. What is the minimum level of equipment availability necessary to keep a combat force effective? • Should be looked at over a system's life cycle (MTBSA may change depending upon durability, overhaul, recapitalization, and planned replacements).

Sortie Reliability/Task Reliability	Definition: Probability that a system can execute a sortie or task once initiated (probability of no failures from time of sortie departure/task initiation until sortie/task completion that would prevent the system from continuing and executing the mission)
	• This is an important metric for periods in which little (e.g., only computer reset) or no maintenance is possible. Serves as another measure of combat power potential.
	• Examples: Will a missile complete its flight without experiencing a malfunction? Can a helicopter reach and attack a target without breaking down? Can a tank cross the line of departure and assault an enemy position without experiencing a critical operating failure?
	• A function of five elements: MTBCF, the length of the sortie or pulse, the operating profile during the sortie or pulse, quick fault-correction capability, and the ability to anticipate and correct probable faults prior to the sortie or pulse.
	• Should be looked at over a system's life cycle (MTBSA may change depending upon durability, overhaul, recapitalization, and planned replacements).

Refit capability or refit period length	Refit capability
	  Definition: Percent of force that can be brought from NMC to MC status during a refit period.
	  Assumption: Refit period length.
	Refit period
	  Definition: Length of refit period necessary to provide a given level of refit capability.
	  Assumption: Refit capability.

	• Or both could be used without a predetermined assumption of the other.
	• Refit activities can potentially include incomplete repairs on system aborts, deferred maintenance of failures or combat damage that occurred during pulses, and anticipatory maintenance. Deferred maintenance can include NMC events that were not repaired (system unavailable during remainder of pulse after failure) and essential function failures (EFF). An EFF is any incident or malfunction which causes inability to perform or a degradation in performance in one or more of the mission-essential functions of a system, but its use can continue during the pulse. System degradation must be of sufficient significance that maintenance to

	remedy the degradation is required before undertaking subsequent missions. Mission-affecting failures give rise to unscheduled maintenance actions. • A critical assumption will be the degree to which broken or damaged end items will be recovered during combat pulses. What will happen to equipment that cannot be repaired by the maneuver force's organic maintenance capability? What will happen to equipment within the force's repair capability that cannot be repaired before the highly mobile force performs another extended maneuver? Will immobilized equipment be blown up in place? Will it be evacuated by like systems (called self-recovery capability)? If so, how will this affect combat power during pulses? Or will there be a handful of recovery vehicles? The answers to these questions could play a critical role in the benefits of refit and the type of work performed during refit. In the extreme case, refit could consist primarily of end item replacement, prognostic maintenance, services, and deferred maintenance on still-mobile equipment, with all immobilized equipment being left behind.
Pulse length/refit period	Definition: Pulse length/refit period length. • Measures the portion of time in which a combat force is available for operations. • Serves as a measure of efficiency with regard to providing combat power to the commander for a deployed force. • Can be thought of as a measure related to campaign effectiveness.
Key assumptions for mission effectiveness metrics	• Pulse length (days). • Pulse profile (mileage, operating hours, tasks). • Sortie and task profiles (mileage, operating hours, tasks). • Expected availability at start of campaign (and initial availability for subsequent pulses). • Administrative lead time (maintenance wait time, coordination delays, part wait time, recovery time). • Reliability degradation over time (a function of the relationship between MTBSA and time and overhaul and recapitalization plans).

Self-sufficiency	Enables objective force operational concepts by making possible nonlinear operations with noncontiguous lines of communication.
Pulse length (Constraint or metric)	Definition: Length of time over which a combat force can operate without any resupply of spare parts or maintenance support from units that are not part of the combat force. Could be defined in terms of days or equipment usage.
Maintenance footprint	From the PA_O goals, refit assumptions, the self-sufficiency goal, reliability requirements, combat damage rate assumptions, and maintainability requirements, the Army can determine the maintenance capacity in terms of personnel and equipment necessary at each echelon. Alternatively, these capacity requirements could be fixed if it is desired to constrain footprint to a certain level, and then one would derive one or more of the other requirements.
Number of maintainers (by echelon) Alternative: Maintenance ratio (MR) (by echelon)	• The personnel and their vehicles serve as a footprint driver for the sustainment resources (water, food, fuel, food service personnel, medical personnel, force protection, etc.) necessary to support them. • MR definition: maintenance hours/operating hours. • MR is a function of reliability and maintainability. It provides benefit by serving as a relative measure of supportability to compare systems. However, it does not directly tie to operational needs. For example, the Army could elect to man some units at a level below that indicated by the "local" or echelon MR with the acceptance of temporary maintenance queues (e.g., provide sufficient maintainers in the combat force to maintain a Min PA_O but not to have capacity to complete all repairs). • MR is independent of the usage level in the operating profile (but not the type of usage), whereas the number of maintainers and the resulting consequences are dependent upon the total operating profile.
Weight and cube of maintenance equipment and resources (by echelon)	• The personnel and their vehicles as a footprint driver for the sustainment resources (water, food, fuel, food service personnel, medical personnel, force protection, etc.) necessary to support them. • The weight and cube of maintenance equipment is a deployment footprint driver.

Life Cycle Cost to Maintain	Definition: Net present cost of maintenance over the expected *fleet* life to include any of the following applicable categories and other significant special costs for a given system: • Initial spare parts provisioning. • Annual military personnel cost. • Annual civilian maintainer cost. • Annual maintenance contract cost (nondepot). • Annual depot maintenance cost (organic and nonorganic). • Planned recapitalization costs. • Annual net spare parts cost. • Investment, maintenance, upgrade, and replacement of special tools and test equipment. • Technical data packages. • Post production sustainment and software support. • Infrastructure change requirements. • Could also include design-driven costs where design decisions made solely to improve reliability or maintainability increase cost. This could include component or subsystem redundancy, more robust components, failure prevention sensors, new materials, and prognostic or diagnostic sensors.

Reliability	Reliability is critical to all four overarching goals for two reasons: its effect on a force's ability to accomplish missions and its effect on the resources, in terms of cost and footprint, required to restore and sustain critical weapon systems. While critical failures are of most interest to operators because they can affect mission accomplishment, logisticians are also concerned with noncritical failures because every type of failure produces resource demands: direct and indirect labor, spare parts, transportation, facilities, and training.
Mean Time Between System Aborts (MTBSA)	Definition: Mean time or mileage between system aborts (SA) (new or like-new condition) • A System Abort is an incident that, due to its severity, would cause a system not to start a mission, to be withdrawn from a mission, or be unable to complete a mission. System Aborts give rise to Essential Unscheduled Maintenance Demands. • A key driver of mission effectiveness, footprint, self-sufficient pulse length requirements.

	• Should include inherent or true equipment failures, operational failures "induced" by operators or maintainers, and perceived, but false, failures. Robust designs, though, are also less prone to operator- and maintainer-induced failures—this can be thought of as error proofing. Reliable built-in tests will minimize false failures.
Mean Time Between Essential Function Failures (MTBEFF)	Definition: Mean time or mileage between essential function failures (EFF) (new or like-new condition). • The difference between MTBEFF and MTBSA consists of unscheduled maintenance actions that should be completed during refit (in addition to any SA failures deferred or not completed during the pulse).
Mean Time Between Unscheduled Maintenance Actions (MTBUMA) (by echelon)	Definition: Mean time or mileage between unscheduled maintenance actions (UMA) (new or like-new condition) by echelon. • A key driver of total logistics footprint and life cycle cost. • MTBSA is a subset of MTBEFF, and MTBEFF is a subset of MTBUMA. • Includes inherent or true equipment failures, operational failures "induced" by operators or maintainers, and perceived, but false, failures. Robust designs, though, are also less prone to operator- and maintainer-induced failures—this can be thought of as error proofing. Reliable built-in tests will minimize false failures. • To fully understand and account for the effect of reliability on how resource requirements must be distributed across the logistics system, one needs to divide MTBM metrics into measures by maintenance echelon.
Mean Time Between Scheduled Maintenance Actions (MTBSMA) (by echelon)	Definition: Mean time or mileage between scheduled maintenance actions (SMA) (new or like-new condition) by echelon. • A key driver of total logistics footprint and life cycle cost for echelons of maintenance above operator/crew. • Operator/crew scheduled maintenance actions affect available operating time or potentially MTBSA if not properly executed during a pulse. • Measured separately from MTBUMA, because they put different types of demands on the logistics system, enabling different types of solutions. • To the extent that scheduled maintenance can be smoothed, it reduces workload peaks, which can reduce the necessary maximum maintenance

	capacity. Scheduled maintenance also improves force design flexibility, because it can be executed by shared, nonunit resources (for scheduled maintenance actions above operator/crew level). • To fully understand and account for the effect of reliability on how resource requirements must be distributed across the logistics system, one needs to divide MTBM metrics into measures by maintenance echelon.
Maintainability	Maintainability encompasses factors that affect the resources (amount and distribution across the force) and time needed to complete repairs—including diagnosis and actual work—and capabilities that enable the logistics system to keep failures from affecting operations.
Fraction of Faults Successfully Predicted (FFSP)	Definition: Number of NMC faults predicted with sufficient warning to complete a replacement before a pulse with the fault prediction isolated to the LRU or SRU to replace/(Total number of NMC faults + Number of incorrect NMC event predictions). • Prognostics provide value by enabling the logistics system to anticipate and correct faults in order to avoid failures during combat operations, thus enhancing mission effectiveness. • For prognostics to be valuable, a significant portion of the faults must be predictable. • FFSP is a function of fraction of faults predictable (FFP), the false alarm rate (FAR), and the fault isolation ratio (FIR). FFP is the percentage of the total population of deadlining faults that can be predicted. FAR is the percentage of predictions that are wrong. FIR is the percentage of predictions that identify the exact LRU or SRU to replace.
Fraction of Faults Successfully Diagnosed (FFSD) by automation	Definition: (For faults that should be detected by built-in tests (BIT)/on-board diagnostics (OBD) or by off-system test, measurement, and diagnostic equipment (TMDE)), Number of NMC faults detected and isolated to one LRU or SRU for replacement/(Number of NMC faults + false NMC indications). • Measures the effectiveness and value of automated diagnostics (BIT/OBD and TMDE). • FFSD is a function of fraction of faults detected (FFD), the false alarm rate (FAR), and the fault isolation ratio (FIR). FFD is the percentage of the total population of deadlining faults that can be

	detected out of the population of faults that occur on components with BIT. FAR is the percentage of predictions that are wrong. FIR is the percentage of fault indications that identify the exact LRU or SRU to replace.
Mean Time to Repair (MTTR)	Definition: Average elapsed maintenance work time (often called "wrench-turning time"), which includes diagnosis. • MTTR is affected by how components and subsystems, whichever represents the desired level of replacement, are packaged within the total system. How easy are they to get to (accessibility)? Are they plug-in, plug-out? How many and what types of fasteners are required? How heavy is each part? What special knowledge is necessary? How effective are troubleshooting procedures? • Key assumption is maintainer productivity driven by training and skill levels.
Maintenance Man-hours Per Unscheduled Maintenance Action (MMH/UMA) (by echelon)	Definition: Average hours necessary to complete an unscheduled repair, by echelon. • If only one maintainer can work on a job, then it equals the time to repair. • Together MMH/UMA (for echelons within a combat force), the number of maintainers (for within a combat force), and the MTBSA drive maintenance wait time and thus affect mission effectiveness. • MMH/UMA is affected by how components and subsystems, whichever represents the desired level of replacement, are packaged within the total system. How easy are they to get to (accessibility)? Are they plug-in, plug-out? How many and what types of fasteners are required? How heavy is each part? What special knowledge is necessary? How effective are troubleshooting procedures? • Key assumption is maintainer productivity driven by training and skill levels.
Maintenance Man-hours Per Scheduled Maintenance Action (MMH/SMA) (by echelon)	Definition: Average hours necessary to complete a scheduled repair, by echelon. • At the operator/crew level, affects availability for mission accomplishment. If time to complete needed tasks is not provided, MTBSA may be affected. • With MTBSMA is a key driver of maintainer requirements (for echelons above operator/crew). • Key assumption is maintainer productivity driven by training and skill levels.

Unscheduled Maintenance Distribution (UMA distribution)	Definition: Percentage of deadlining UMAs that can be repaired by crews, other combat force mechanics, and echelons above combat force. • Key assumption is maintainer training and skill levels by echelon. • For example, if crews are highly trained, they can repair a larger percentage of faults, reducing both the overall need for maintainers as well as those in the maneuver force.

Fleet Life Cycle Management	The actual MTBSA for determining PA_O metrics should be a function of the "new/like-new" MTBSA, reliability degradation assumptions, and the following life expectancy metrics (i.e., how often and to what degree a system can be expected to be brought back to like-new condition).
Time to recapitalization	Definition: Planned years between fleet recapitalization events. • Must be accompanied by outline recapitalization plan for use in life cycle cost estimate.
Overhaul limit	Definition: Time or usage between overhauls or condition-based overhaul limit (e.g., inspection criteria). • Must be accompanied by estimated overhaul costs for use in life cycle cost estimate.
Fleet life expectancy	Definition: Number of years the fleet is expected to be in the force. • In conjunction with other life expectancy requirements, enables the determination of an estimate of the number of replacements, overhauls, and recapitalization events that will occur over the fleet life.
Replacement/retirement limit	Definition: Number of years/usage before end item replacement. • Can be used as an alternative or in conjunction with overhaul/recapitalization.

Supply Support	
Combat force fill rate	Definition: Percent of deadlining parts requests during combat pulses that can be satisfied by combat force spare parts inventory. • With controlled exchange and maintenance resources (crews, maintainers, equipment), drives the repairs that can be executed during a combat pulse.

Wholesale backorder rate	Definition: Percent of requests to wholesale that cannot be immediately filled. • Key factor in combat force inventory replenishment and refit capability.
Percent of parts unique	Definition: Percentage of parts unique to the end item within a combat force. • This affects the cost of the combat force fill rate requirement.
Number of end item floats (by echelon)	Definition: Number of floats positioned with each echelon. • When part of the combat force, they influence mission effectiveness in terms of pulse A_O metrics. • When they can be provided to a combat force during a refit period, they affect refit capability.
Key assumptions	• OCONUS distribution speed, which is a key factor in combat force inventory replenishment and refit capability. • Communication effectiveness of combat pulse faults to higher echelons of supply and maintenance, which is a key factor in having resources ready for refit.

BIBLIOGRAPHY

Adler, Allen, Deputy Director DARPA Technology Office, "DARPA Technologies For Future Combat Systems" (Briefing), January 11, 2000.

AF Instruction 10-601, *Mission Needs and Operational Requirements Guidance and Procedures*, October 1, 1998.

Aldridge, E.C., Office of the Undersecretary of Defense for Acquisition, Technology, and Logistics, "MEMORANDUM. Performance Based Logistics," February 13, 2002.

The Army Authorization Documents System, Fiscal Year 1999.

The Army Requirements Process Information Briefing, DAMO-FM.

Andrews, Michael, Dr., Deputy Assistant Secretary of the Army for Research and Technology, "Future Combat Systems (FCS) Science and Technology Briefing," FCS Industry Day, January 11, 2000.

Army Science Board FY2000 Summer Study Final Report (DRAFT), *Technical and Tactical Opportunities for Revolutionary Advances in Rapidly Deployable Joint Ground Forces in the 2015–2025 Era*, Support and Sustainment Panel Report—Draft, September 2000, Department of the Army, ASA(ALT).

Army Working Capital Fund Supply Management, Army FY99 Reapportionment Request: FY00–01 Budget Estimate, September 15, 1998.

"The Army's CS/CSS Transformation: Executive Summary," Briefing, January 21, 2000.

Assistant Secretary of the Army Financial Management and Comptroller, "The Army Budget: FY01 President's Budget," February 2000.

CJCSI 3170.01A, *Requirements Generation System.*

Comanche Helicopter Analysis of Alternatives (AOA) Logistics Impact Analysis (LIA).

"Concepts for the Objective Force," United States Army White Paper, 2001.

Department of the Army 2001 Procurement Program FY01 President's Budget, February 2000.

Department of the Army FY 2001 Budget Estimate Operation and Maintenance, Army National Guard, February 2000.

Department of the Army FY 2001 Budget Estimate Operation and Maintenance, Army Reserve, February 2000.

Department of the Army FY 2001 Budget Estimate Operations and Maintenance Army, Volume 1: Justification of OMA Estimates for FY 2001.

Department of the Army FY 2001 Budget Estimate Operations and Maintenance Army, Volume 2: Data Book.

Department of the Army, Army Working Capital Fund FY 2001 Budget Estimates, February 2000.

DoD Directive 5000.1, *The Defense Acquisition System*, October 23, 2000.

DoD Instruction 5000.2, *Operation of the Defense Acquisition System*, Change 1, January 4, 2001.

DSMC—Acquisition Logistics Guide, Third Edition, Defense Systems Management College: Fort Belvoir, VA, December 1997.

Dumond, John, Rick Eden, Douglas McIver, and Hyman Shulman, *Maturing Weapon Systems for Improved Availability at Lower Costs*, Santa Monica, CA: RAND, MR-338-A, 1994.

Force Development Requirements Determination, TRADOC Pamphlet 71-9, Department of the Army Training and Doctrine Command, November 5, 1999.

FORMIS, FY1999 Army Personnel Database, Defense Manpower Data Center.

Future Combat Systems Solicitation (FINAL), July 18, 2000.

FY1998 Contract Action Data File, Directorate for Information Operations and Reports, Washington Headquarters Services, Department of Defense, *http://web1.whs.osd.mil./peidhome/guide/procoper.htm*.

Guidelines for the Army Requirements Oversight Council (AROC), Enclosure to memo Shinseki, Eric, Chief of Staff United States Army, Memorandum, SUBJECT: Approval of Army Warfighting Requirements, March 19, 2001.

Mandatory Procedures for Major Defense Acquisition Programs (MDAPs) and Major Automated Information System (MAIS) Acquisition Programs, Interim Regulation, DoD 5000.2-R, January 4, 2001.

May, Ingo, Dr., Future Combat Systems Technologies Briefing: Summary of Army Programs, January 11, 2000.

Military Composite Standard Pay and Reimbursement Rates Department of the Army for Fiscal Year 1999, Tab K-2.

Morris, Seymour, et al., *Reliability Toolkit: Commercial Practices Edition: A Practical Guide for Commercial Products and Military Systems Under Acquisition Reform*, Rome, NY: Reliability Analysis Center, IIT Research Institute, 1995.

National Research Council, *Reducing the Logistics Burden for the Army After Next: Doing More with Less*, National Academy Press: Washington, DC, 1999.

Objective Force: Organization and Operations Concept, Final Draft, 5 February 2001.

Operational Requirements Document Format, Enclosure to Memorandum Eric Shinseki, Chief of Staff United States Army, Memorandum, SUBJECT: Approval of Army Warfighting Requirements, March 19, 2001.

Page, Thomas F., Combat Arms Director, HQ TRADOC, FCS Industry Day Requirements Briefing, January 11, 2000.

Peltz, Eric L., Marc L. Robbins, Patricia Boren, and Melvin Wolff, *Diagnosing the Army's Equipment Readiness: The Equipment Downtime Analyzer*, Santa Monica, CA: RAND, MR-1481-A, 2002.

Reliability and Maintainability (R&M) Requirements Rationale (RRR) for the Force XXI Battle Command Brigade and Below (FBCB2) System, ATCD-SRE-K (70), October 23, 1995.

Reliability as a KPP (Briefing), DAMO-FD, August 2, 2000.

Reliability, Availability, and Maintainability (RAM) Rationale Report (RRR) for the Deployable Universal Combat Earthmover (DEUCE), October 8, 1993.

Shinseki, Eric, Chief of Staff United States Army, Memorandum, SUBJECT: Approval of Army Warfighting Requirements, March 19, 2001.

Stanley, William L., and John L. Birkler, *Improving Operational Suitability Through Better Requirements and Testing*, Santa Monica, CA: RAND, R-3333-AF, 1986.

Study of the Development and Application of Supportability Metrics to Army Acquisition Programs, Office of the Deputy Chief of Staff for Logistics, DALO-SMR, Department of the Army, August 28, 2000.

Van Fosson, Marion, Program Manager Future Combat Vehicle, FCS Industry Day Program Overview Briefing, January 11, 2000.

Zanini, Daniel R., Deputy Chief of Staff for Combat Developments, United States Army Training and Doctrine Command, Memorandum, SUBJECT: Policy for Updating Operational Requirements Documents (ORDS), May 22, 1998.